a Penguin Book

Seven Hundred Penguins

PENGUIN BOOKS

Published by the Penguin Group
Penguin Books Ltd, 80 Strand, London WC2R ORL, England
Penguin Group (USA) Inc., 375 Hudson Street, New York, New York 10014, USA
Penguin Group (Canada), 90 Eglinton Avenue East, Suite 700, Toronto, Ontario, Canada
M4P 2Y3 (a division of Pearson Penguin Canda Inc.)
Penguin Ireland, 25 St Stephen's Green, Dublin 2, Ireland (a division of Penguin Books Ltd)
Penguin Group (Australia), 250 Camberwell Road, Camberwell, Victoria 3124, Australia
(a division of Pearson Australia Group Pty Ltd)
Penguin Books India Pvt Ltd, 11 Community Centre, Panchsheel Park, New Delhi – 110 017,
India
Penguin Group (NZ), 67 Apollo Drive, Rosedale, North Shore 0632, New Zealand
(a division of Pearson New Zealand Ltd)
Penguin Books (South Africa) (Pty) Ltd, 24 Sturdee Avenue, Rosebank, Johannesburg 2196,
South Africa

Penguin Books Ltd, Registered Offices: 80 Strand, London WC2R ORL, England

www.penguin.com

First published 2007
1

Set in Adobe Sabon and Berthold Akzidenz Grotesk
Designed by David Pearson
Colour reproduction by MDP Ltd, Wiltshire, England
Printed in Italy by Graphicom Group, Vicenza, Italy

ISBN: 978-0-141-03188-0

Introduction

This is a book of books. Gathered here on these seven hundred pages is an enormously eclectic assortment of Penguin covers that are beautiful, stimulating and entertaining. The diversity and spirit of this anthology comes in part from the organic selection process: we wanted this to be a book of favourites, so members of staff from Penguin's offices around the world were asked to nominate their favourite covers for inclusion. We also wanted to represent the broadest range of styles, so while thousands of the famous Penguin three-panel ('tri-part') covers were used from 1935 to the early fifties, in this book you'll only find about a dozen. From the early fifties on, Penguin's front covers used illustration and photography in an ever greater variety of ways, and so these are included more liberally.

Most of the covers are British, but there are also inspired covers from Australia, Canada, India, New Zealand and South Africa. Almost all of the British covers have been pulled from Penguin's vast archive in Rugby, where row upon row of shelves hold a copy of almost every British Penguin book ever published. Special thanks go to in-house Penguin cover designer (and designer of this book) David Pearson, for spending more than a few days sifting through the endless aisles at Rugby, locating the books people had suggested and selecting his own favourites in the process. Not so much a labour of love as a calling of compulsion: David has always championed quintessentially Penguin design and was the motivating force behind *Penguin by Design* (2005), the design critique by Phil Baines published to celebrate Penguin's seventieth anniversary.

While we're still too close to more recent covers to judge them objectively, we can now confidently look back at the twentieth century with a cool sense of detachment and see those books with fresh eyes. What we find is that most of these covers still look superb, and we can marvel at the skills of the people involved who created the more timeless covers. There are many fans of the elegant and perfectly measured covers designed by Jan Tschichold. There are also many admirers of books using arresting illustrations by David Pelham and plenty who enjoy the visual witticisms of Derek Birdsall. Needless to say, we are all drawn to countless innovative mutations of Romek Marber's remarkable Penguin-saving grid template, which will fascinate more than just design fanatics. Not forgetting, of course, the contributions from hundreds of other leading designers and artists over the years.

But flicking through this book it's often the least expected things that catch your eye, and often, without any formula at all, a cover manages to capture a moment even though many aspects of it are not necessarily 'well designed' or even coherent. It's these covers that, while often transcending all design logic, somehow sum up a book and its resonance perfectly. What's exciting about *Seven Hundred Penguins* is that these kinds of covers have made it in. We wanted the covers included here to be memorable, and who is to say that that is not the most effective and important criterion for the design of a book cover?

Inevitably, while putting together this book there have been heated debates about what makes a good or bad book cover. What we've realized is that there is no one-size-fits-all formula for a great cover. What some people love, others hate. The curious twist is that the older a paperback is, the greater its appeal. Why should this be the case? And why is it that so many *Penguin* paperbacks in particular have the power to evoke such warmth and affection?

It's likely that some of these books act as conduits for our own memories. These fragile – almost disposable – books have travelled through our lives with us; they are the same objects that we held with younger hands, or we cherished as gifts, or we picked up in significant places. They are a repository of memories, and *Seven Hundred Penguins* is a place of memories we've all experienced, the constant being the little (or in some cases not so little) Penguin logo.

An individual book can reveal idiosyncrasies about its owner, through scribbled notes or turned-down pages. Collectively, books disclose a lot about a person – it's always intriguing in people's homes to run an eye along their bookshelves and see what is divulged: a complete set of Sartre; a burst of Muriel Spark; a curious range of D. H. Lawrence and an unexpected interest in herbs and ethics all together on their shelves. It can tell you more than years of late-night conversation.

So you can read *Seven Hundred Penguins* as a selection of Penguin's bookshelf. All the books selected here were produced in the period running from Penguin's birth in 1935 to the year 2000, illustrating some of what we've published, designs we've fostered, designers and artists who have worked with us. Consequently *Seven Hundred Penguins* uniquely assembles some of the most compelling paperback designs of the twentieth century.

The consistent output of memorable covers comes from a deep-rooted design imperative that has been the backbone of Penguin's covers from day one. Considered design is a quality a publisher can never regret, and we still reinforce it's importance wholeheartedly today. Some covers shown here are less familiar than others, but it's exciting that there are so many unexpected charming choices. Discovering the lesser-known ones is not unlike finding treasure; you can't beat unearthing superb old books like these. I love going to the book market under the last arch of Waterloo Bridge, just across the Thames from the Penguin office, the perfect spot to stumble across such surprising gems. It's also the ideal place to witness the affection people display for a lovingly worn Penguin paperback. People bunch up around the Penguin section, politely jostling, peering past each other at the rows of orange, green and blue, brushing their fingers over the coordinated spines and uncoordinated logos. And as the covers flap in the river breeze (somehow keeping clear of gusting showers), you'll see people tenderly pick up a book or two, holding them protectively as they pay.

Paperbacks like these are intrinsically vulnerable – they cannot, and will not, last forever. Despite being relatively common (in some cases millions have been printed, in others only a few thousand), these books yellow and crumble as each year passes and so their numbers diminish. Yet looking again recently at an old copy of James Joyce's *Dubliners* (it's now somewhere in among these pages), it's incredible how well paperbacks can survive. The paper, yellowing even the first time I read it, is even browner now, and the dog-eared cover somehow affirms the fragility of being, and yet the whole thing is intact. For a paperback to survive twenty or thirty years is a decent achievement. For paperbacks to survive fifty, sixty or seventy years, as many shown in this book have, well, that practically makes them worthy of antique status, and still they can be had, from a second-hand bookshop, for the price of a packet of cigarettes.

But as much as we love these paperbacks and feel like they are a permanent part of our lives (as well as our parents' and grandparents' lives), they cannot be permanent, and maybe in a few decades they will only be found in museums of the long-forgotten twentieth century. So enjoy them again here in *Seven Hundred Penguins*, but also enjoy the ones you have at home. Brush blindly past those shelves no more, and love your long-forgotten Penguins as the little works of art they really are.

Jim Stoddart

A note on image reproduction

In the main, the paperbacks reproduced on these pages are either A format (181 mm x 111 mm) or the larger B format (198 mm x 129 mm), the two most common book sizes within the publishing industry. All are shown at 90% of their actual size.

Although necessary for legibility, image retouching and colour correction have been kept to a minimum to ensure a faithful reproduction of the original.

Acknowledgements

We wish to thank the following people for their very generous support: Alistair Richardson; Helen Conford; Stefan McGrath; Richard Duguid; Seyhan Esen; Katja Kiebs; Marina Maher; Sue Osborne; Clare Skeats; Steve Hare; Phil Baines; Kristen Harrison; Adam O'Riordan; Michael Hawkes; Elizabeth Ockleshaw; Scott Sherman; and special thanks to Jonathan Pearson.

a Penguin Book 3/6

The Birdcage

John Bowen

a Penguin Book 3/6

Frenchman's Creek

Daphne du Maurier

Alcoholism

Neil Kessel and Henry Walton

Alexa

Andrea Newman

a Pelican Original 7/6

The Worker and the Law

K. W. Wedderburn

EMPLOYER

EMPLOYEE

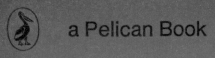

a Pelican Book   9'6

The Pacifist Conscience

Edited by Peter Mayer

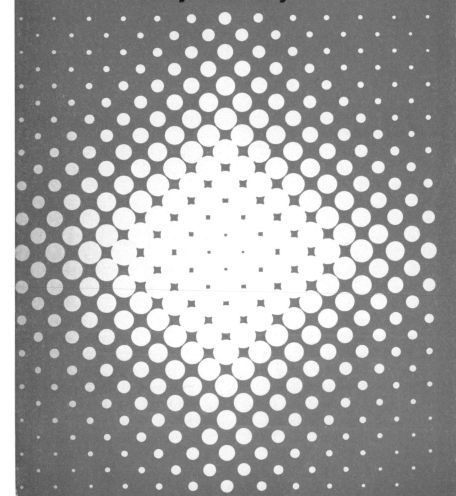

Peter De Vries
The Blood of the Lamb

Lord Peter views the body

Dorothy L. Sayers

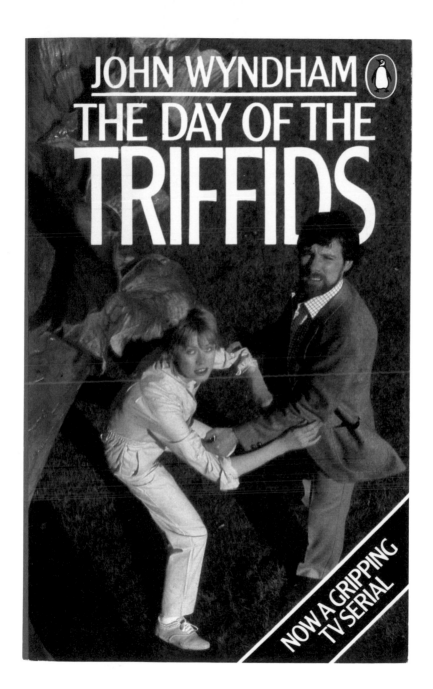

JOHN WYNDHAM

THE DAY OF THE
TRIFFIDS

NOW A GRIPPING TV SERIAL

PENGUIN BOOKS

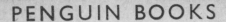

DENEYS REITZ

Commando

Memoirs of the Boer War by one who fought the British as a guerilla soldier under Botha, Smuts and their colleagues, to become later one of the architects of the Union of South Africa and its official representative in London. This account of the exploits of the mobile columns of picked fighters who opposed the British so vigorously fifty years ago, and bequeathed their name to the picked men who played so gallant a part in World War II, is a thrilling narrative of the romance and adventure of war which has become a classic.

BIOGRAPHY

Complete **2/-** Unabridged

The Penguin Book of Welsh Verse

Translated with an introduction
by Anthony Conran

7/6

FACING UP TO MODERNITY
PETER L. BERGER

THE
GERMAN
LEBENSRAUM

ROBERT E. DICKINSON

THE FORCES BOOK CLUB

Penguin Modern Classics   3/6

Virginia Woolf

The Death of the Moth

and Other Essays

Ellery Queen
The Blue Movie Murders

a Pelican Original 3'6

sexual deviation

Anthony Storr

Graham Greene

The Quiet American

Poetry of the Thirties
Introduced and Edited by Robin Skelton

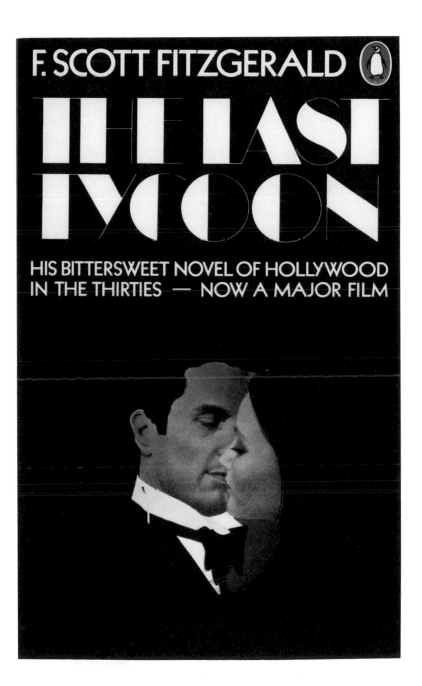

F. SCOTT FITZGERALD

THE LAST
TYCOON

HIS BITTERSWEET NOVEL OF HOLLYWOOD
IN THE THIRTIES — NOW A MAJOR FILM

a Penguin Book   3'6

Agents and Patients

Anthony Powell

A Pelican Book

God Is
No More

Werner and Lotte Pelz

PENGUIN BOOKS

Aldous Huxley

—

ANTIC
HAY

—

A Novel

COMPLETE 65c UNABRIDGED

The Company She Keeps

Mary McCarthy

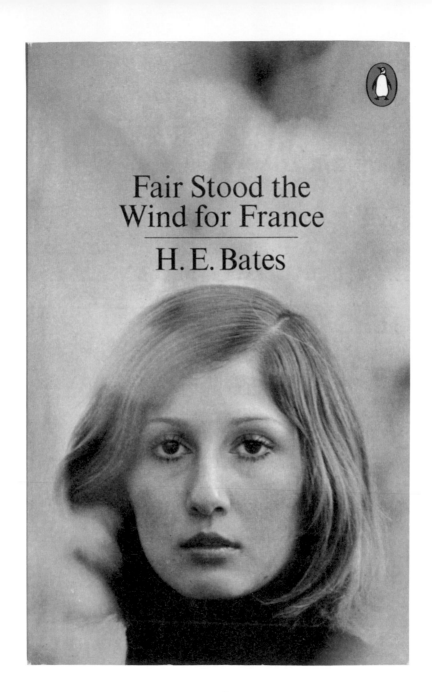

Fair Stood the
Wind for France

H. E. Bates

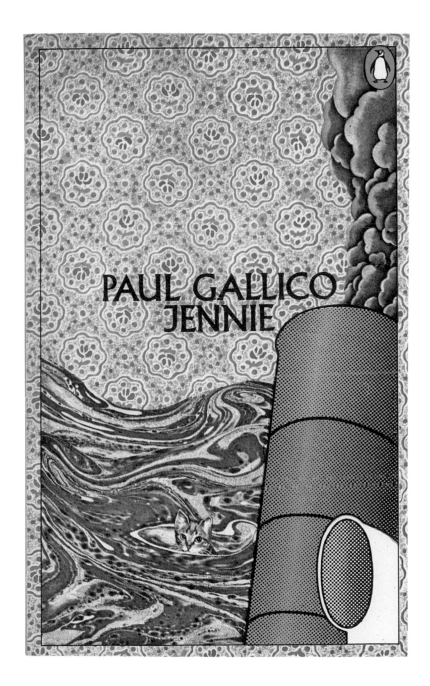

PAUL GALLICO
JENNIE

a Pelican Book   3/6

Aspects of the Novel

E. M. Forster

BEETHOVEN

*Symphony No. 9 in
D minor*

PENGUIN SCORES 28 · 8/6

a Penguin Book 4'6

The Parasites

Daphne du Maurier

Penguin Science Fiction

H.G.Wells

John Berger

*The novel which won
the 1972 Booker Prize*

G.

J. B. Priestley

The Good Companions

34

A PENGUIN BOOK

Honor Blackman's Book of Self-Defence

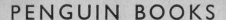

PENGUIN BOOKS

T H E

Journals

O F

A R N O L D

B E N N E T T

Selected and edited by
FRANK SWINNERTON

3/6

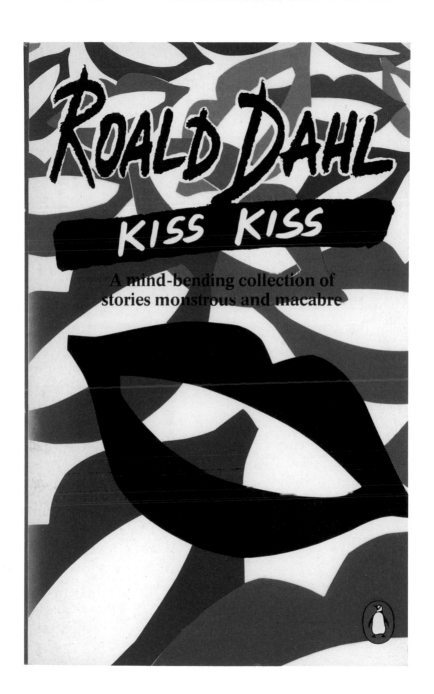

ROALD DAHL

KISS KISS

A mind-bending collection of
stories monstrous and macabre

8/6

Mile End
Greenwich
The Zoo
Smithfield
Pall Mall
Camberwell
Rte Eleven

**Nairn's
London
Ian Nairn**

St Paul's
Twickenham
Temple
Wapping
Ham Common
Lululand
Queenhythe

CUV 217 C

Penguin Science Fiction

5/-

The Man in the High Castle

Philip K. Dick

HEALTH OF THE FUTURE

Aleck Bourne

a Penguin Book 3/6

An American Romance

Hans Koningsberger

THE JUDGE & HIS HANGMAN

FRIEDRICH DÜRRENMATT

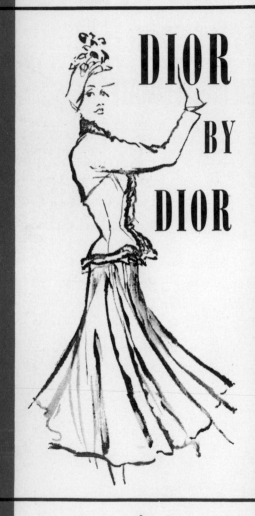

DIOR
BY
DIOR

COMPLETE **2/6** UNABRIDGED

LAURENS VAN DER POST
VENTURE
TO THE INTERIOR

Thomas Mann

The Holy Sinner

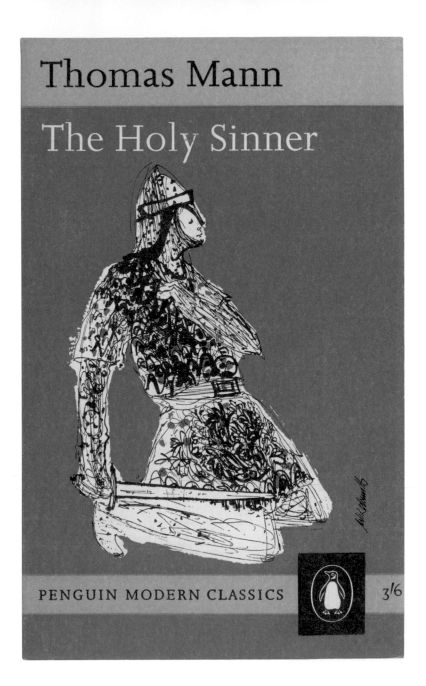

PENGUIN MODERN CLASSICS

3/6

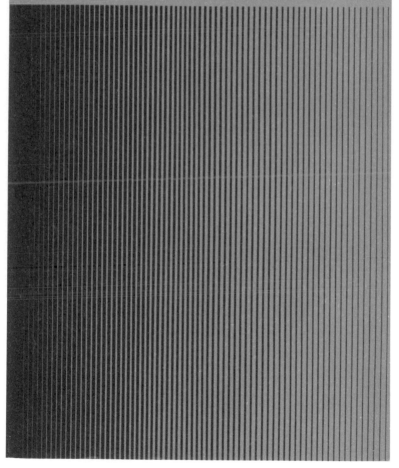

6/-

Ethics

P. H. Nowell-Smith

FACE TO FACE
VED MEHTA

The autobiography of a young Indian blind from childhood

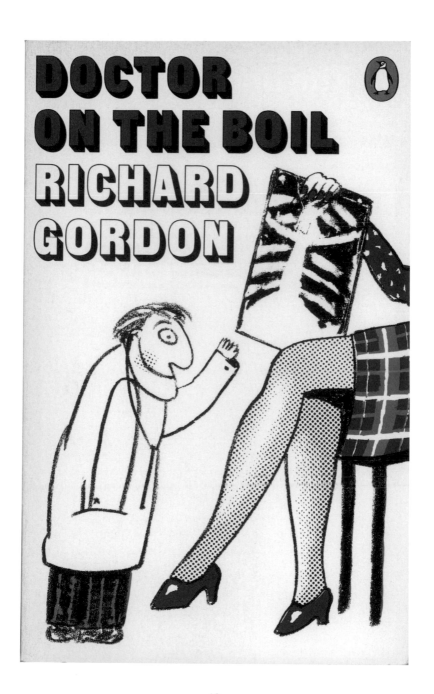

DOCTOR ON THE BOIL
RICHARD GORDON

PENGUIN BOOKS

The Gathering Storm

THE FIRST VOLUME OF

The Second World War

WINSTON S. CHURCHILL

COMPLETE AND UNABRIDGED

7/6

SAUL BELLOW

WINNER OF THE 1976 NOBEL PRIZE FOR LITERATURE

HERZOG

a Pelican Original 7/6

MAGNETISM

E.W.LEE

A WOLF
ADVENTURING
Jean Forton

4/-

a Penguin Book 2/6

Stop at Nothing

John Welcome

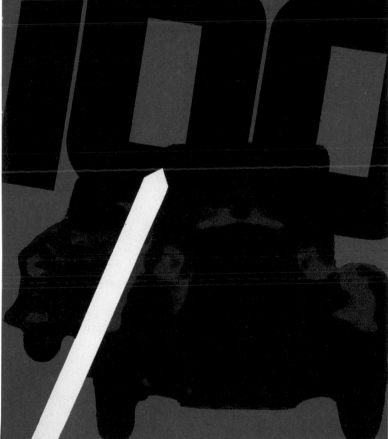

Listen to danger

3/6 dorothy eden

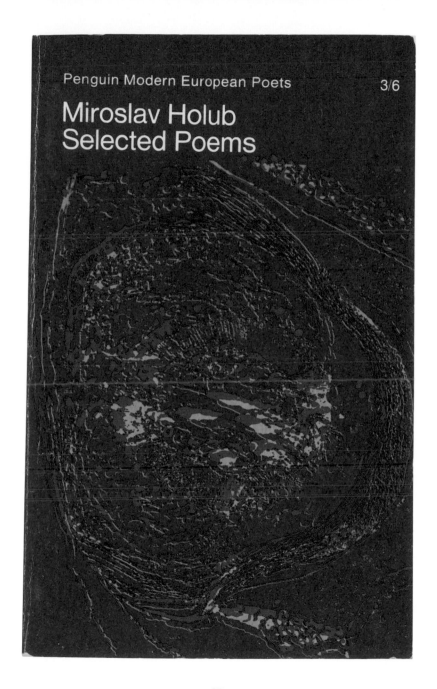

Penguin Modern European Poets   3/6

Miroslav Holub
Selected Poems

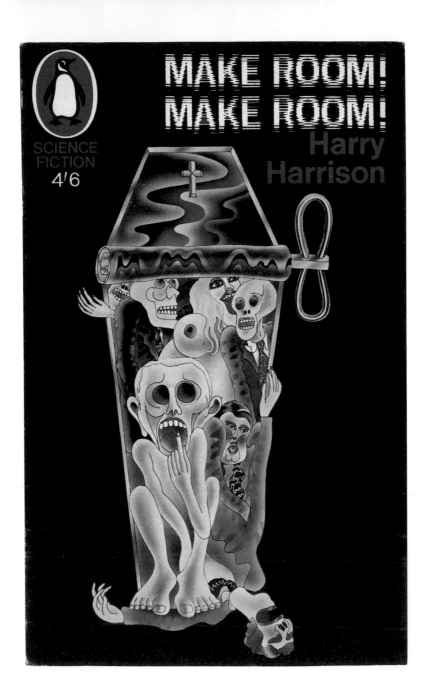

a Penguin Book 5/-

The Boy in the Bush

D. H. Lawrence and M. L. Skinner

The World in
the Evening
Christopher
Isherwood

5/-

The New English Bible

OLD TESTAMENT

APOCRYPHA

NEW TESTAMENT

a Pelican Original

The Psychology of Play

Susanna Millar

A B C
D E F
G H I
K L M

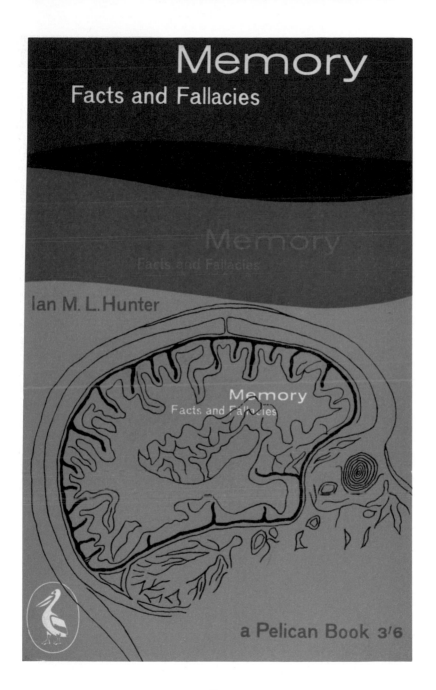

Memory
Facts and Fallacies

Ian M. L. Hunter

a Pelican Book 3/6

Penguin Modern Classics

6'-

Bertolt Brecht

Threepenny Novel

EDNA
O'BRIEN
back to innocence,
and Ireland
A PAGAN
PLACE

E·M·FORSTER

A PASSAGE
TO INDIA

a Pelican Original

Family Planning

Edited by Jean Medawar
and David Pyke

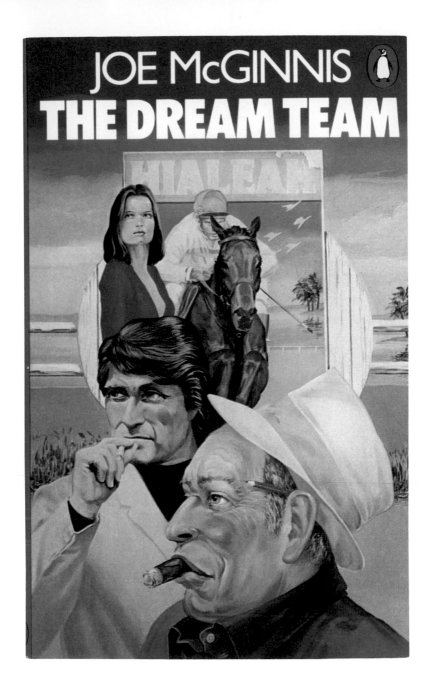

JOE McGINNIS

THE DREAM TEAM

Günter
Grass

DOG
YEARS

PENGUIN BOOKS

Victor Gollancz

A
YEAR
OF
GRACE

Passages chosen and arranged to express
a mood about God and man

3/6

LEN DEIGHTON

BILLION-DOLLAR BRAIN

A PENGUIN BOOK

Axe
Ed McBain
An 87th Precinct Mystery

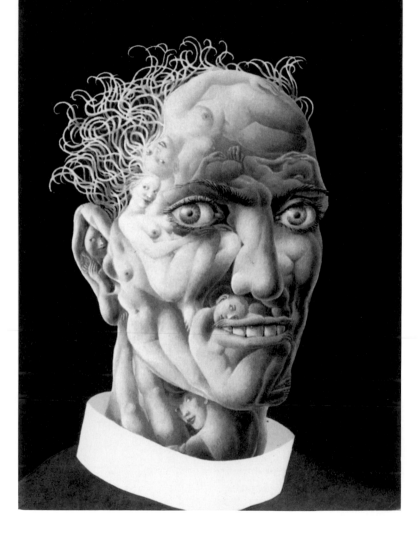

JOHN UPDIKE

'An erotic *tour de force*' – *The Times*

A MONTH OF SUNDAYS

Penguin Modern Classics

E. M. Forster
A Room with a View

ERLE STANLEY GARDNER

THE CASE OF
THE BAITED HOOK

FABIAN

PENGUIN BOOKS 2/6

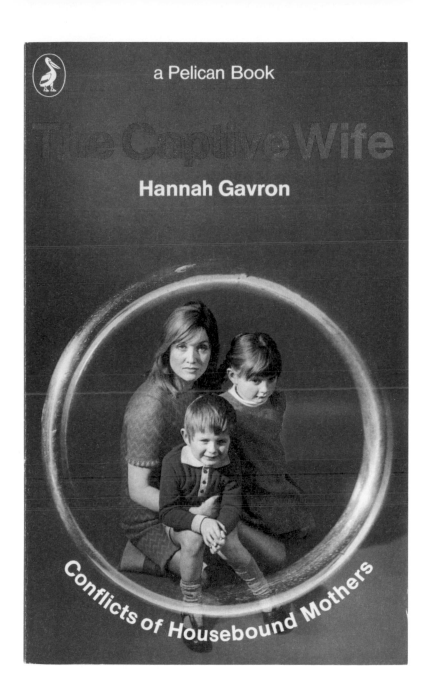

a Pelican Book

The Captive Wife

Hannah Gavron

Conflicts of Housebound Mothers

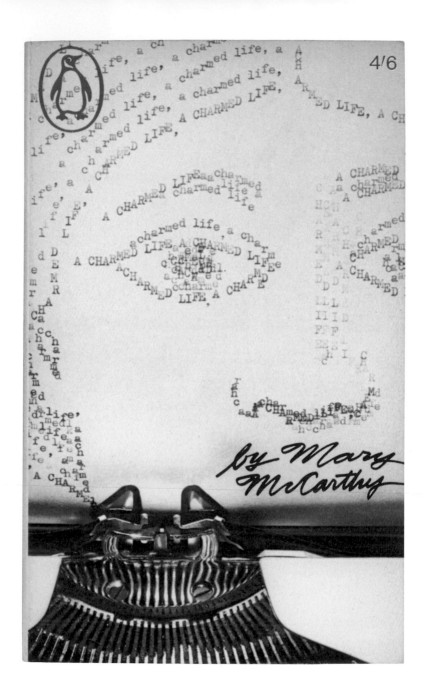

4/6

a charmed life, a charmed life, a charmed life, a charmed life, a charmed life, A CHARMED LIFE, A CH

A CHARMED LIFE, a charmed charmed life a charmed life, a charm A CHARMED LIFE A CHARMED LIFE A CHARMED LIFE, A CHARMED LIFE, A CHAR

A CHARMED CHARMED

by Mary McCarthy

Bridge to the Sun

Gwen Terasaki

PENGUIN BOOKS

4/-

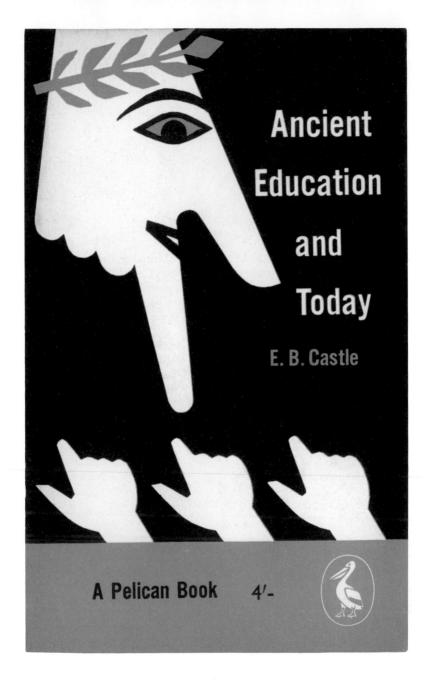

Ancient
Education
and
Today

E. B. Castle

A Pelican Book   4'-

Bandoola

J. H. WILLIAMS

'Touches a peak as high as that
achieved by *Elephant Bill*' –
Daily Telegraph

A Penguin Book 4/-

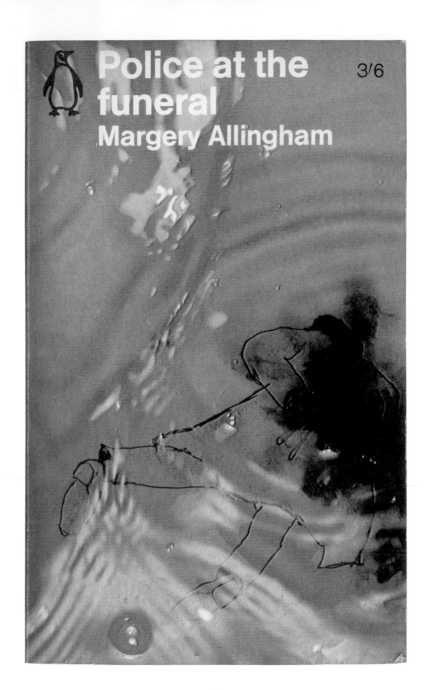

Police at the
funeral

Margery Allingham

3/6

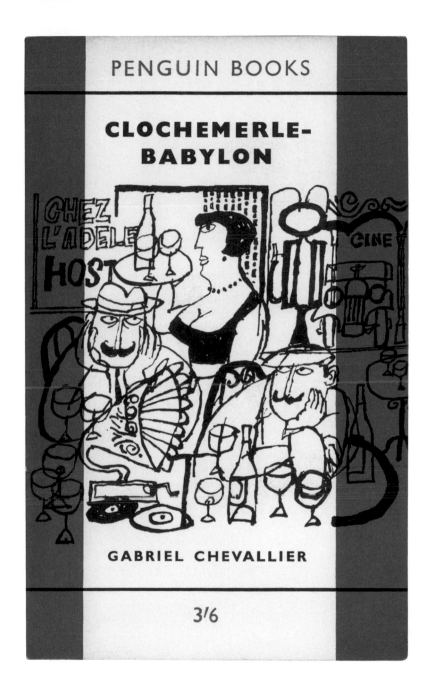

PENGUIN BOOKS

CLOCHEMERLE-BABYLON

GABRIEL CHEVALLIER

3/6

The Colossus of Maroussi

HENRY MILLER

'Marvellous things happen to one in Greece—
marvellous *good* things which can happen
to one nowhere else on earth.'

a Penguin Book   **3/6**

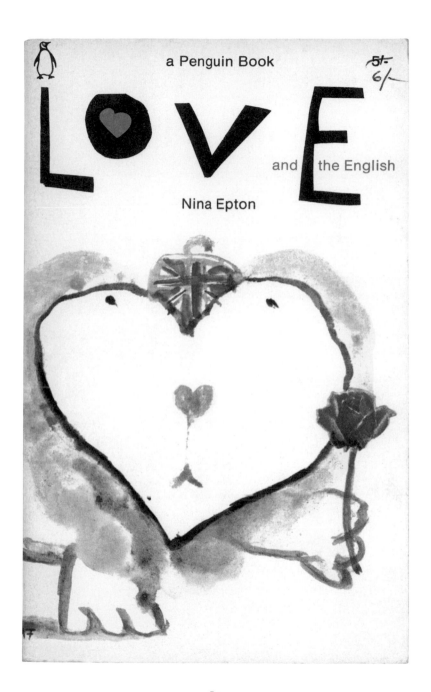

a Penguin Book

5/-
6/-

LOVE

and the English

Nina Epton

A PENGUIN SPECIAL

Edward Glover

THE
PSYCHOLOGY
OF
FEAR
AND
COURAGE

PEARLS ARE A NUISANCE
RAYMOND CHANDLER

Man and Automation

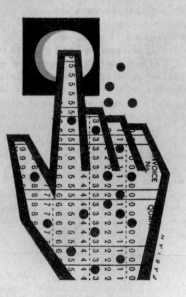

L. LANDON GOODMAN

PUT OUT THE LIGHT

LIGHT

A THRILLER

ETHEL LINA WHITE

complete **PENGUIN BOOKS** unabridged

THE
CRUEL SEA
THE GREAT NOVEL OF WAR AT SEA
MONSARRAT

a Penguin Book   3'6

The Quiet American

Graham Greene

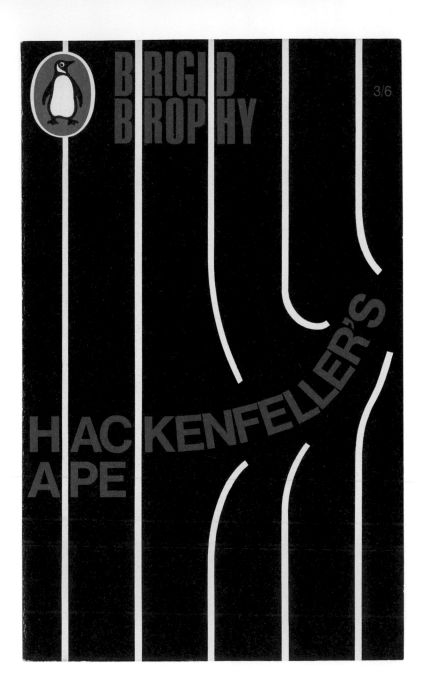

BRIGID
BROPHY

3/6

HACKENFELLER'S
APE

NOW A MAJOR PARAMOUNT PICTURE STARRING ROBERT REDFORD AND MIA FARROW

The Great Gatsby

F. Scott Fitzgerald

Writers from the Other Europe
General Editor: PHILIP ROTH

THE FAREWELL
PARTY

MILAN KUNDERA
Introduction by Elizabeth Pochoda

Penguin Modern Poets 26
Dannie Abse,
Michael Longley,
D. J. Enright

What I'm going to do, I think

L. Woiwode

Kingsley
Amis
Take a Girl
Like
You

DE VALERA

Sean O'Faolain

A New Biography

Written specially for
this series

PENGUIN BOOKS

maigret
sets a trap

SIMENON
MAIGRET

Daphne du Maurier
Jamaica Inn

PENGUIN
BOOKS

PRICE
1/3

OLD JUNK

FICTION

FICTION

H. M. TOMLINSON

COMPLETE   UNABRIDGED

I Should Have Stayed Home

Horace McCoy

3/6

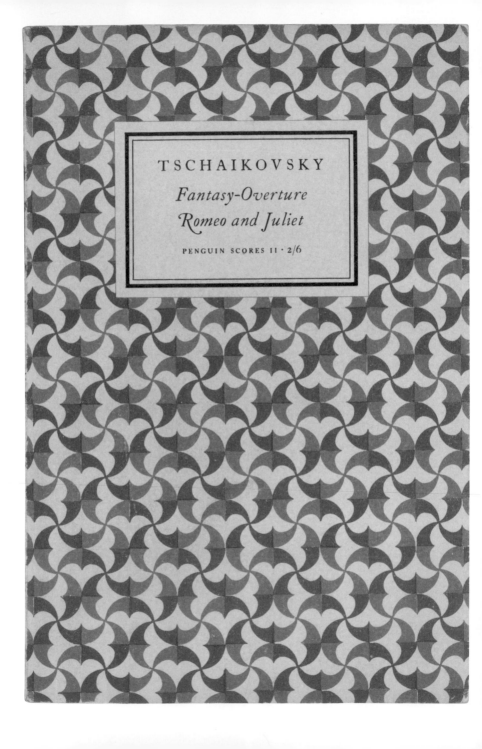

TSCHAIKOVSKY

Fantasy-Overture
Romeo and Juliet

PENGUIN SCORES 11 · 2/6

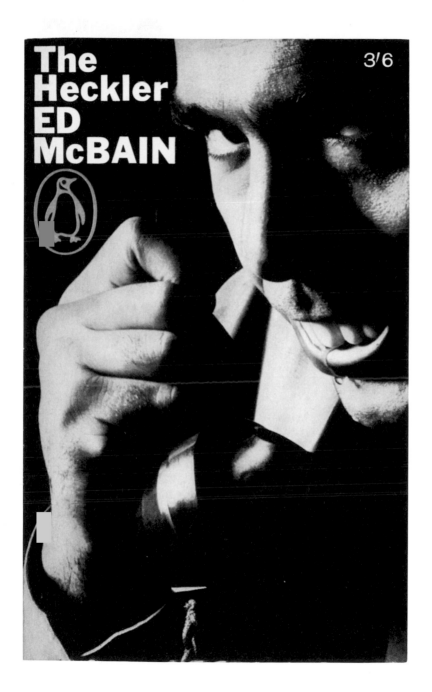

The
Heckler
ED
McBAIN

3/6

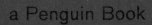 a Penguin Book

 2'6

The Long March

William Styron

Herzog

By
Saul
Bellow

5/-

Bertolt Brecht
Threepenny Novel

MEDICINE TODAY

Wonder drugs, deep-freeze surgery, and other topics explained with pictures

David Margerson

A Penguin Book 5s

a Penguin Book

5/-

THE ORIGINS OF THE SECOND WORLD WAR

A. J. P. Taylor

'This is an almost faultless masterpiece, perfectly proportioned, perfectly controlled' – *Observer*

A Night of Errors
of Errors
Michael Innes

THE
RISE
OF THE
MERITOCRACY 1870-2033

Michael Young

A Pelican Book 3/6

AUBREY MENEN

THE PREVALENCE OF
WITCHES

A. GAMES.

PENGUIN BOOKS 2/6

The Drunken Forest
Gerald Durrell

GEORGE ORWELL

NINETEEN EIGHTY-FOUR

a Pelican Original

The Menstrual Cycle

Katharina Dalton

a Penguin Book 3/6

A Severed Head

Iris Murdoch

PENGUIN BOOKS

TAKE
THESE MEN

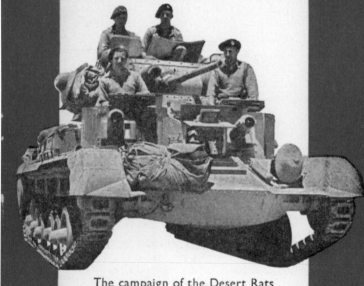

The campaign of the Desert Rats
from 1940 to 1943

CYRIL JOLY

COMPLETE **3/6** UNABRIDGED

HEINRICH BÖLL

Winner of the Nobel Prize for Literature 1972

GROUP PORTRAIT WITH LADY

ThePenguinFeiffer

5/-

MARGARET
DRABBLE
A SUMMER
BIRD-CAGE

NEW BIOLOGY

PENGUIN BOOKS

2/6

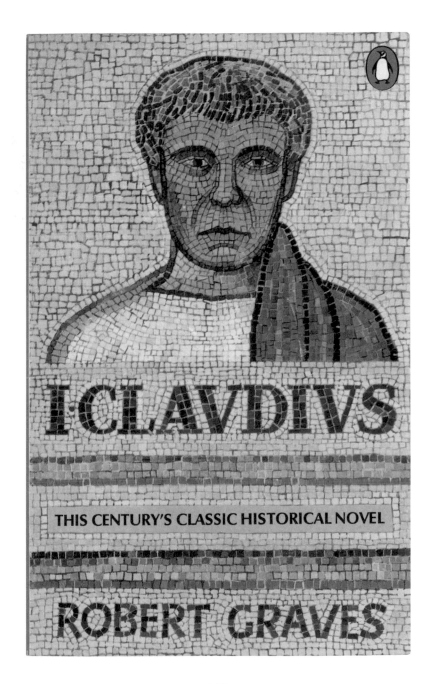

I·CLAVDIVS

THIS CENTURY'S CLASSIC HISTORICAL NOVEL

ROBERT GRAVES

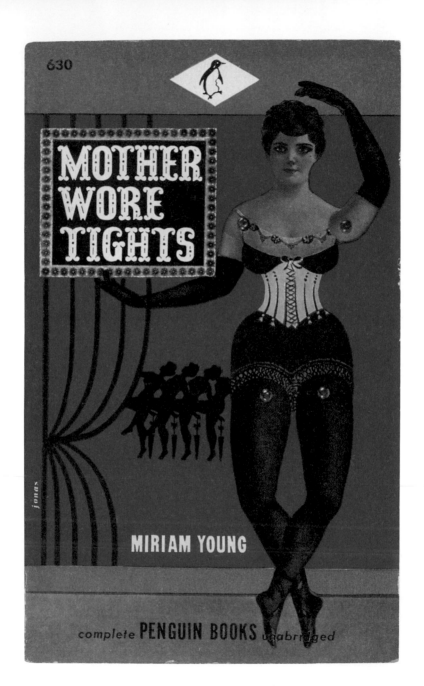

630

MOTHER WORE TIGHTS

jonas

MIRIAM YOUNG

complete PENGUIN BOOKS unabridged

Penguin Modern Classics   5'-

The Sound and the Fury

William Faulkner

A Dictionary of Electronics

S. Handel

Penguin
Reference
Books
7'6

ALAN JAY LERNER

My Fair Lady

EDNA
O'BRIEN
A SCANDALOUS
WOMAN
and other stories

Emma Lathen

MURDER MAKES THE WHEELS GO ROUND

This executive's job turned out to be the death of him...

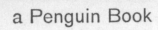

a Penguin Book 3/6

My Turn to Make the Tea
Monica Dickens

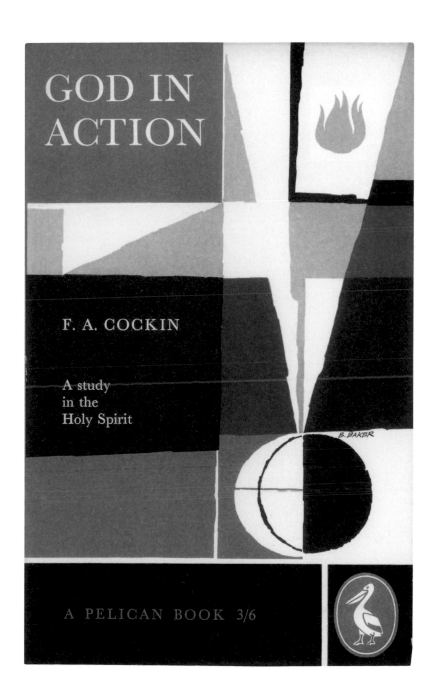

GOD IN ACTION

F. A. COCKIN

A study
in the
Holy Spirit

B. BAKER

A PELICAN BOOK 3/6

HOPJOY WAS HERE 3'6
Colin Watson

Who put Hopjoy
in the Acid Bath?

PENGUIN BOOKS

ROOM AT THE TOP

John Braine

Laurence Harvey
as Joe Lampton in the
Romulus film of the book

COMPLETE **2/6** UNABRIDGED

DAYS OF
WINE AND RAGE

Frank Moorhouse

The case of
the rolling
bones

3/6

Erle Stanley Gardner

Vladimir Nabokov

Ada

William Faulkner
The Wild Palms

SPINSTER

Sylvia Ashton-Warner

The book of the Julian Blaustein Film production *Spinster*, starring Shirley MacLaine,
Laurence Harvey, and Jack Hawkins. Released
by Metro-Goldwyn-Mayer

PENGUIN BOOKS   **3/6**

ERLE STANLEY GARDNER

THE D.A. HOLDS
A CANDLE

PENGUIN BOOKS **2/6**

Ernest Hemingway

The Snows of Kilimanjaro

and Other Stories

3/6

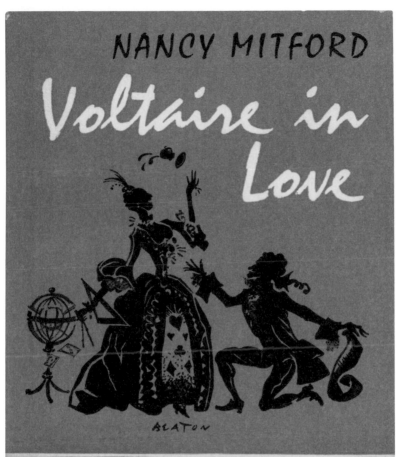

NANCY MITFORD

Voltaire in Love

ALATON

Penguin
Biography

3'6

by the author of
A CLOCKWORK ORANGE

ANTHONY BURGESS

INSIDE MR ENDERBY

PENGUIN
BOOKS

SUNSHINE SKETCHES
OF A LITTLE TOWN

STEPHEN
LEACOCK

COMPLETE

UNABRIDGED

Sweet Dreams
Michael Frayn

Science Fiction

PHILIP K. DICK

Time Out of Joint

The Unpleasant Profession of Jonathan Hoag

Robert A. Heinlein

a Penguin Book

4/-

THE AMERICAN WAY OF DEATH

Jessica Mitford

a Pelican Book

Art and its Objects

Richard Wollheim

Alberto Moravia
Two
Adolescents

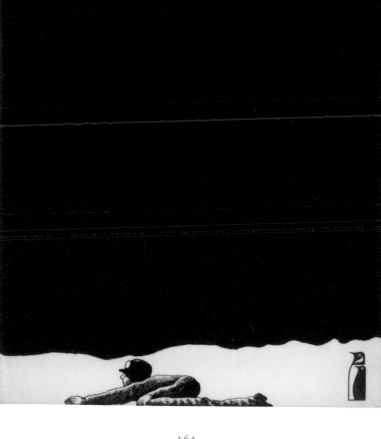

A SPECIAL CASE?

SOCIAL JUSTICE AND THE MINERS
EDITED FOR THE NUM BY JOHN HUGHES and ROY MOORE

AMERICA THE VINCIBLE

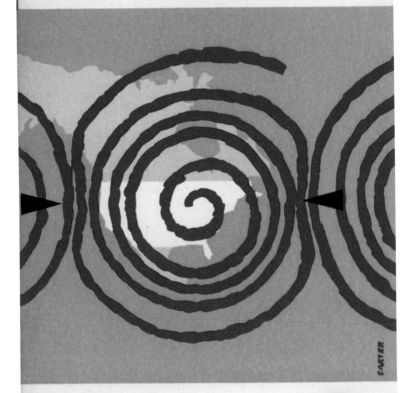

A study of America's role in world affairs by

EMMET JOHN HUGHES

A PENGUIN SPECIAL

3/6

HELTER SKELTER

NOW A DISTURBING FILM

THE MANSON MURDERS
VINCENT BUGLIOSI WITH CURT GENTRY

The Pelican Latin American Library

Edited by M. Kenner and J. Petras

FIDEL CASTRO SPEAKS

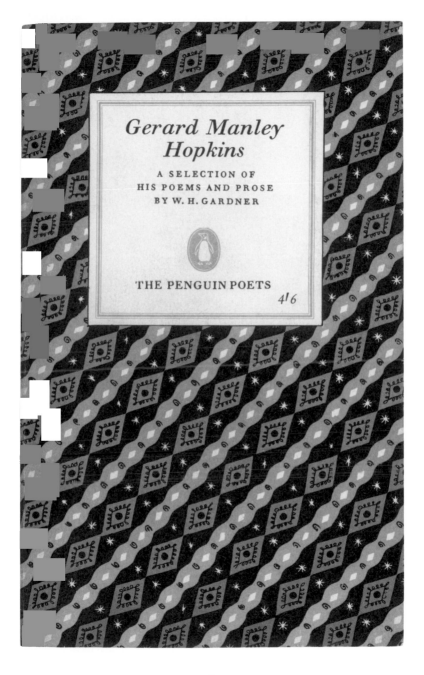

*Gerard Manley
Hopkins*

A SELECTION OF
HIS POEMS AND PROSE
BY W. H. GARDNER

THE PENGUIN POETS

4ˡ6

FRED & GEOFFREY

HOYLE

THE INFERNO

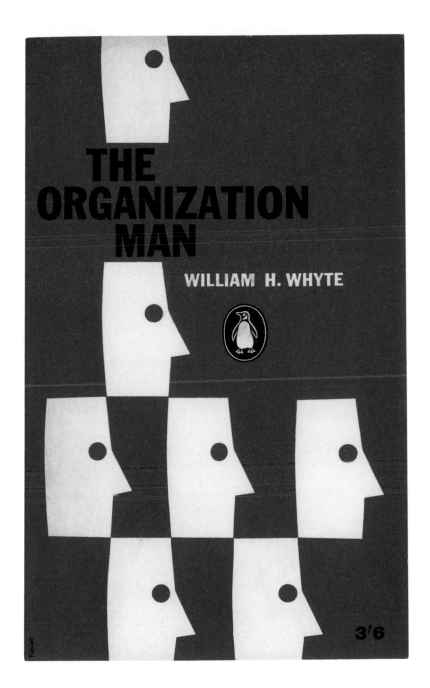

THE
ORGANIZATION
MAN

WILLIAM H. WHYTE

3'6

The Penguin
Cookery Book

a Penguin Handbook

Bee Nilson

6/-

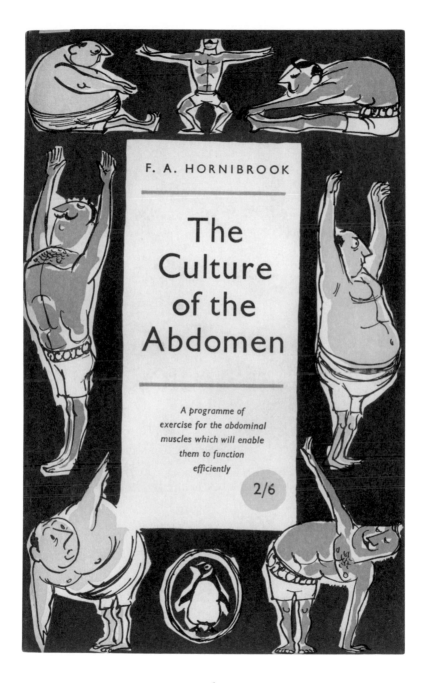

F. A. HORNIBROOK

The
Culture
of the
Abdomen

*A programme of
exercise for the abdominal
muscles which will enable
them to function
efficiently*

2/6

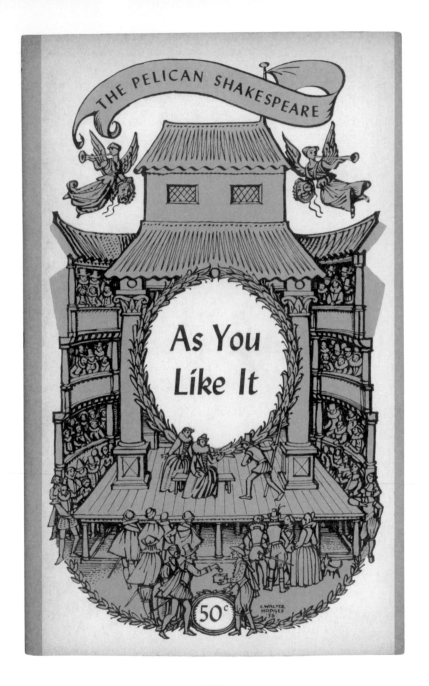

THE PELICAN SHAKESPEARE

As You Like It

50c

C. WALTER HODGES 56

Browning

A SELECTION BY
W. E. WILLIAMS

THE PENGUIN POETS

6/-

PENGUIN REFERENCE

THE PENGUIN

DICTIONARY OF ARCHAEOLOGY

WARWICK BRAY AND DAVID TRUMP

ROBERT IRESON

The Penguin
Car
Handbook

6/-

A
Penguin
Special
by

**Ping-
Chia
Kuo**

One of
the
first
books to
throw
new
light on
the
Chinese
revolution

3/6

CHINA
New Age and New Outlook

Vladimir Nabokov

Lolita

The greatest novel of rapture in modern fiction

THE CONDITION OF ENGLISH SCHOOLING

EDITORS: HENRY PLUCKROSE & PETER WILBY

PELICAN BOOKS

BIRD
RECOGNITION

VOLUME ONE
SEA-BIRDS AND WADERS

JAMES FISHER

2/6

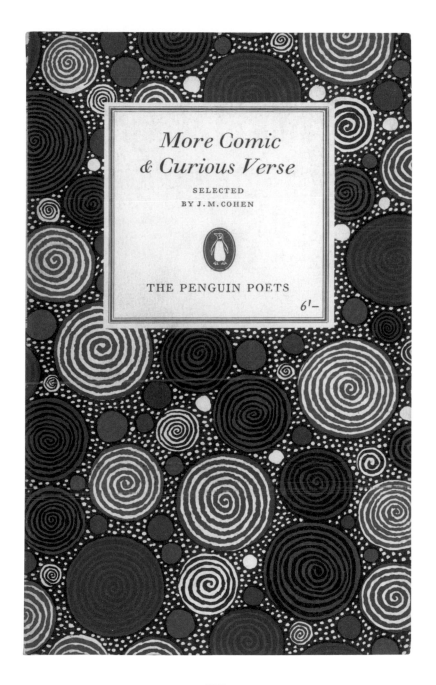

*More Comic
& Curious Verse*

SELECTED
BY J.M.COHEN

THE PENGUIN POETS

6/-

CRIME

The Fourth Stage of Gainsborough Brown
Clarissa Watson

British Poetry since 1945

Edited with an Introduction by
Edward Lucie-Smith

THE PENGUIN

DICTIONARY OF
COMPUTERS

ANTHONY CHANDOR
WITH JOHN GRAHAM AND ROBIN WILLIAMSON

a Penguin Book 3/6

Hurry on Down

John Wain

Stanley Cohen and Laurie Taylor
Escape Attempts
The Theory and Practice of Resistance
to Everyday Life

ANDREW
ROTHSTEIN

A
History
of the
U.S.S.R.

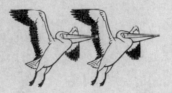

A DOUBLE VOLUME
TWO SHILLINGS AND SIXPENCE

THE FIRST YEAR OF TEACHING

CHARLES HANNAM, PAT SMYTH AND NORMAN STEPHENSON

A PENGUIN HANDBOOK

SOFT FRUIT GROWING

RAYMOND BUSH

a salute to
the great mccarthy
barry oakley

Edward de Bono
The Dog-Exercising Machine
A Study of Children as Inventors

ENDLESS PRESSURE

KEN PRYCE

The Penguin Book of Canadian Verse

Edited by Ralph Gustafson
Revised Edition

John S. Scott

The Penguin Dictionary of

BUILDING

PELICAN BOOKS

AN OUTLINE OF
EUROPEAN
ARCHITECTURE

NIKOLAUS PEVSNER

ERVING GOFFMAN FRAME ANALYSIS

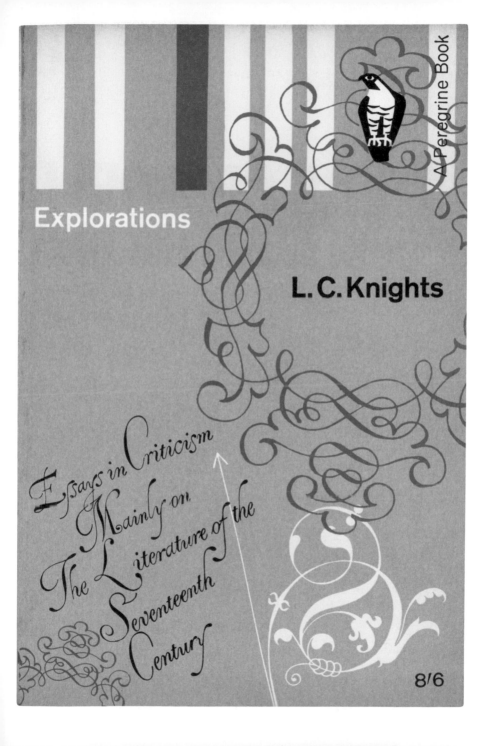

Explorations

L. C. Knights

A Peregrine Book

Essays in Criticism Mainly on The Literature of the Seventeenth Century

8/6

*Colin McEvedy and
Richard Jones*

ATLAS OF WORLD
POPULATION HISTORY

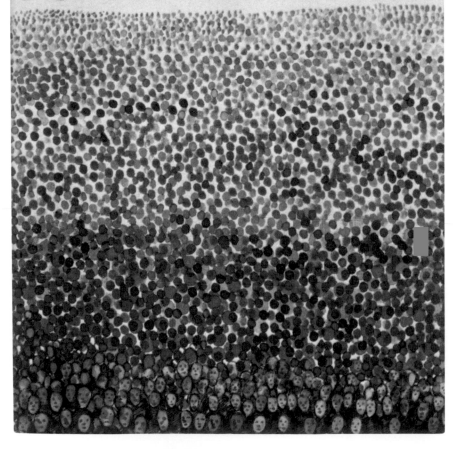

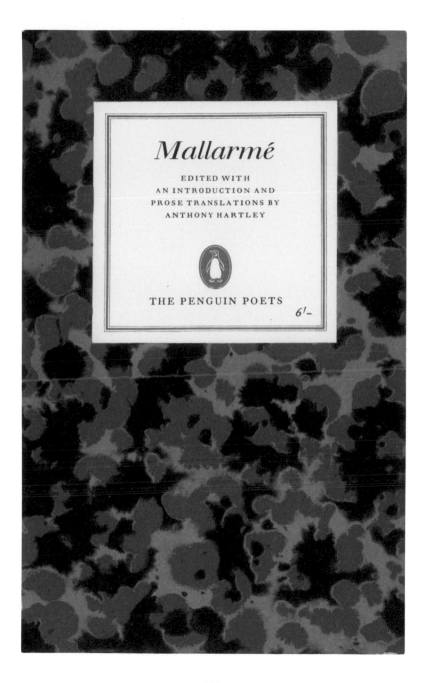

Mallarmé

EDITED WITH
AN INTRODUCTION AND
PROSE TRANSLATIONS BY
ANTHONY HARTLEY

THE PENGUIN POETS

6/-

A Dictionary
of Science

Penguin
Reference
Books

E. B. Uvarov
D. R. Chapman
Alan Isaacs

Revised Edition

5/-

GARDENING THE MODERN WAY

ROY HAY

A Penguin Handbook prepared in conjunction and collaboration with the Royal Horticultural Society

6/-

TREAT YOURSELF TO SEX

A Guide to Good Loving

Paul Brown/Carolyn Faulder

THE BIRTH CONTROL BOOK

The most comprehensive and candid
guide to birth control ever published:

HOWARD I. SHAPIRO

The Nature of
Greek Myths

G. S. Kirk

A *Penguin Special*

NEW SERIES NUMBER TWO

I Choose Peace

K. ZILLIACUS

Bernard Shaw *in the New Statesman* :
'Mr Zilliacus is not a man to be ignored ... He is the only internationally minded member of any note in the House of Commons. He is a man who must be attended to, and his questions answered if another fiasco like that of Versailles and its sequel in 1939-45 is to be averted.'

2/6

a Penguin Book   3/6

The World in Winter

John Christopher

New Penguin Shakespeare

Henry IV, Part 2

PENGUIN SCIENCE OF BEHAVIOUR

BRAIN DAMAGE AND THE MIND

MOYRA WILLIAMS

PELICAN BOOKS

British Herbs

FLORENCE RANSON

1/6

SCIENCE
NEWS 44

PENGUIN BOOKS 2/6

The Atom and the Energy Revolution

A Penguin Special by

NORMAN LANSDELL

2/6

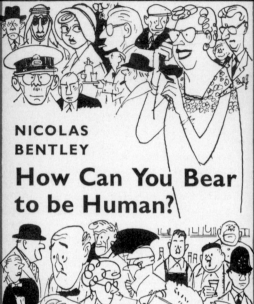

NICOLAS BENTLEY

How Can You Bear to be Human?

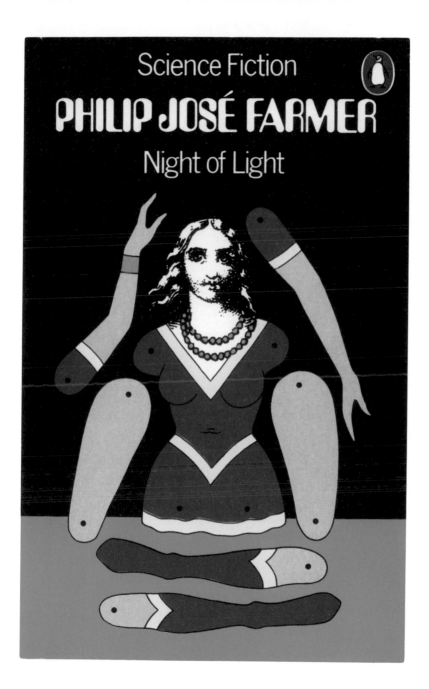

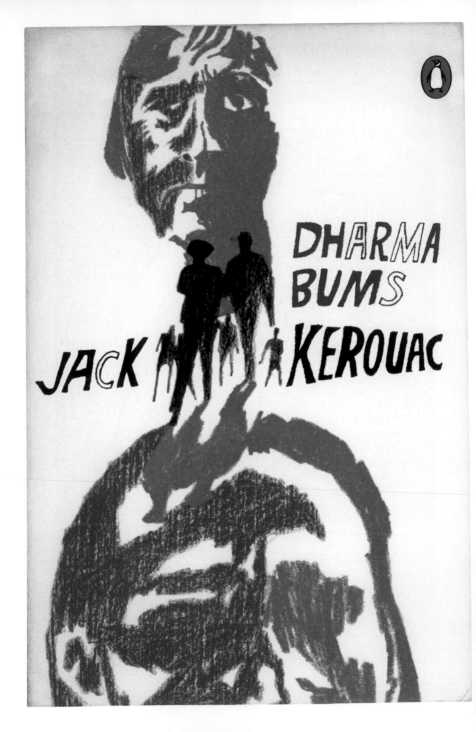

Killer in the Rain
Raymond Chandler

PENGUIN
HANDBOOKS

ARTHUR
CROXTON SMITH

Dogs

A complete guide to
choosing, training, breeding, and
caring for all kinds of dogs,
whether they are kept for
sporting, working, or show
purposes, or simply as pets and
companions

2/6

Interior
Design

7/6

a Penguin Handbook
Diana Rowntree

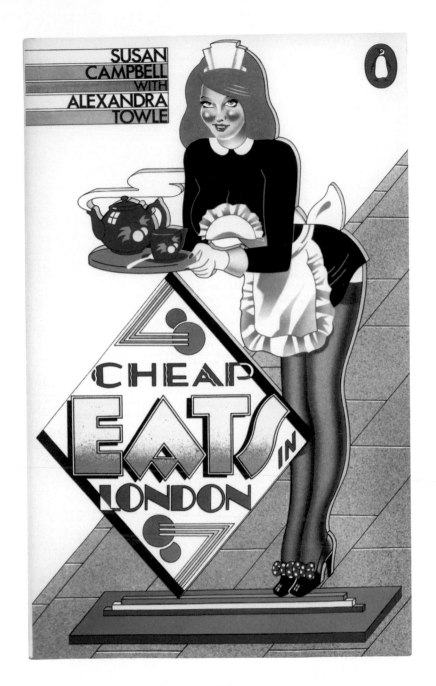

Saul Bellow

HERZOG

Penguin Plays

FAIRY TALES
OF
NEW YORK

J. P. Donleavy

'A chain of theatrical pearls, nourished
by a master of comic dialogue'
KENNETH TYNAN in the *Observer*

2/6

VLADIMIR NABOKOV

Lolita

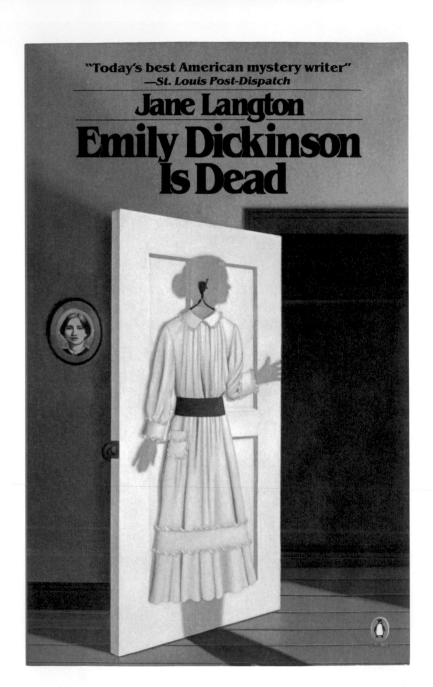

"Today's best American mystery writer"
—*St. Louis Post-Dispatch*

Jane Langton
Emily Dickinson
Is Dead

GRO⌁TH
ECONOMICS

EDITOR: AMARTYA SEN

PENGUIN MODERN ECONOMICS READINGS

Advice your family doctor never gave you...

Dear
Dr HIPPocrates
Eugene Schoenfeld

One Flew Over
The Cuckoo's Nest

Ken Kesey

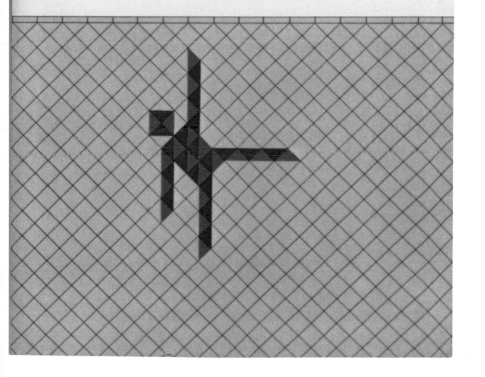

Modern science studies

Modern
Physics

edited by David Webber

GUY de MAUPASSANT

BOULE
DE SUIF

AND OTHER
STORIES

A NEW TRANSLATION BY
H. N. P. SLOMAN

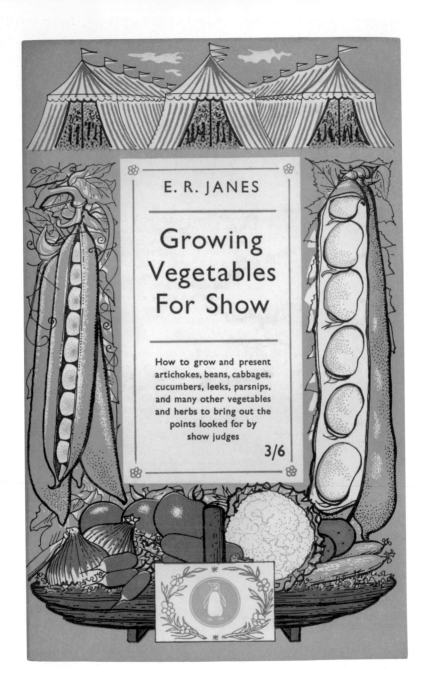

E. R. JANES

Growing Vegetables For Show

How to grow and present
artichokes, beans, cabbages,
cucumbers, leeks, parsnips,
and many other vegetables
and herbs to bring out the
points looked for by
show judges

3/6

FUNDAMENTAL
QUESTIONS
IN PHILOSOPHY

STEPHAN KÖRNER

DOCTOR
in the house
RICHARD
GORDON

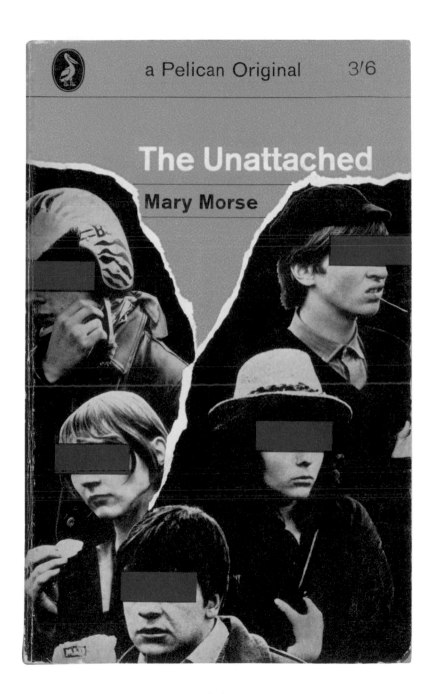

J.K.Galbraith
Economics,
Peace & Laughter

A Contemporary Guide

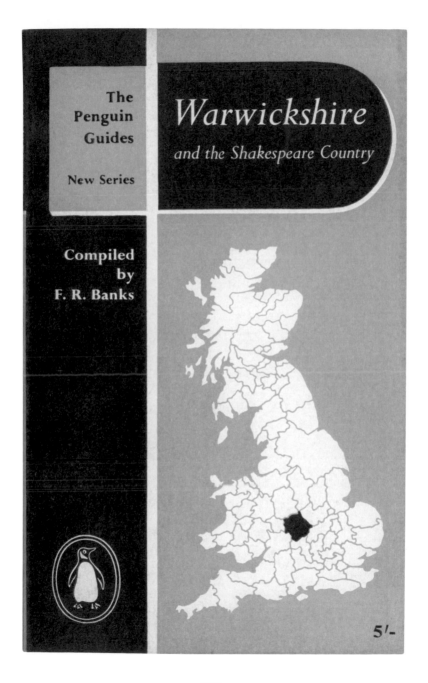

The Penguin Guides

New Series

Warwickshire

and the Shakespeare Country

Compiled by
F. R. Banks

5/-

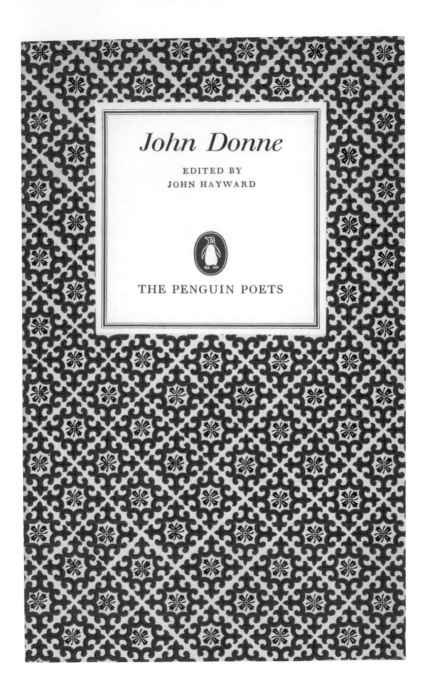

John Donne

EDITED BY
JOHN HAYWARD

THE PENGUIN POETS

KING PENGUIN

PAUL BAILEY

Old Soldiers

IMMIGRATION AND RACE IN BRITISH POLITICS

a Penguin Special   4/6

Paul Foot

KHRUSHCHEV'S
Russia

A PENGUIN SPECIAL BY
Edward Crankshaw

2/6

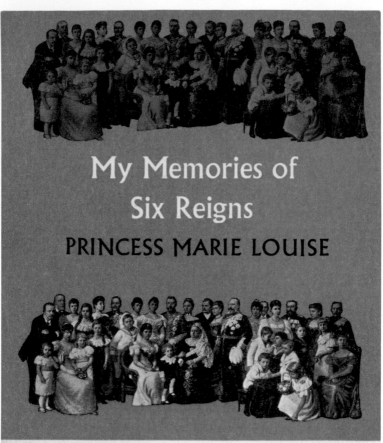

My Memories of
Six Reigns
PRINCESS MARIE LOUISE

Penguin
Biography

4/-

Penguin Crime

3/6

Inspector Queen's Own Case

Ellery Queen

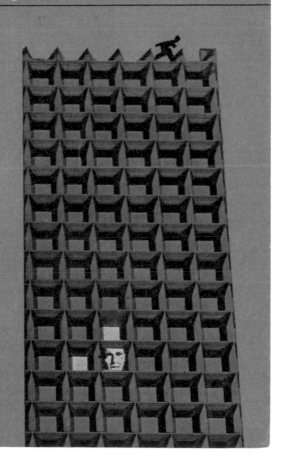

VANCE PACKARD

The Hidden Persuaders

2'6

*An introduction to the techniques of
mass-persuasion through the unconscious*

CARTER

MOZART'S LETTERS

Edited and Introduced by
Eric Blom

Wolfgango amadeo Mozart 1780

Selected from
The Letters of Mozart and His Family
Translated and Annotated by
Emily Anderson

KING PENGUIN

THE OLD BOYS
William Trevor

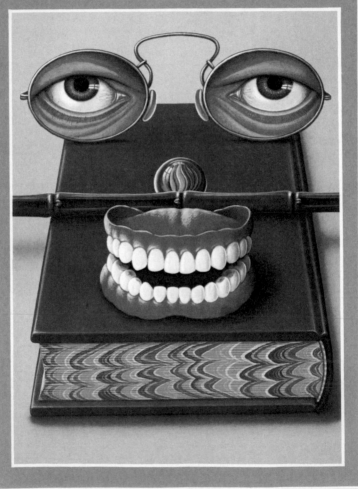

PHYSICS REFERENCE BOOKS **VOLUME ONE**

F.C.FLACK, K.E.GREW, T.W.PREIST, W.G.V.ROSSER

M TION

& UNITS

an Australian Penguin Book 3/6

To the Islands

Randolph Stow

The Quest for Proust

André Maurois

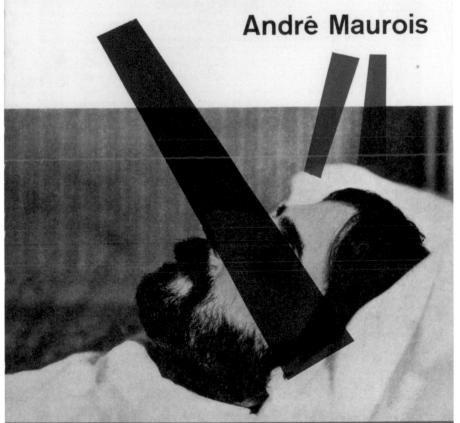

A Peregrine Book

10'6

HOWARDS END

E. M. Forster

4s
20p

A PENGUIN INTERNATIONAL EDITION

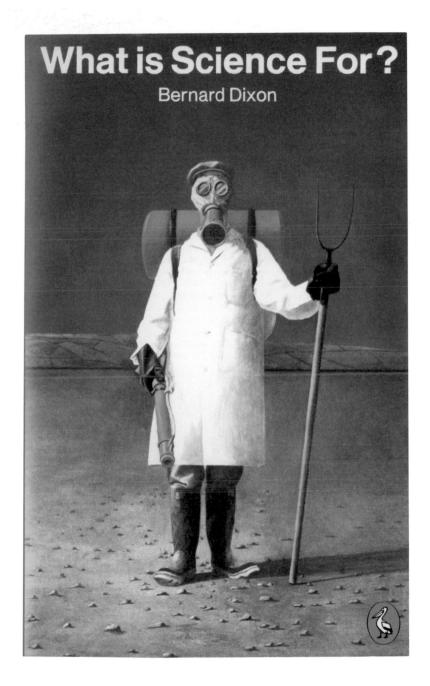

What is Science For?

Bernard Dixon

Great Cities
and Their Traffic

J. Michael Thomson

PENGUIN EDUCATION SPECIALS

THE SPECIAL CHILD

BARBARA FURNEAUX
SECOND EDITION

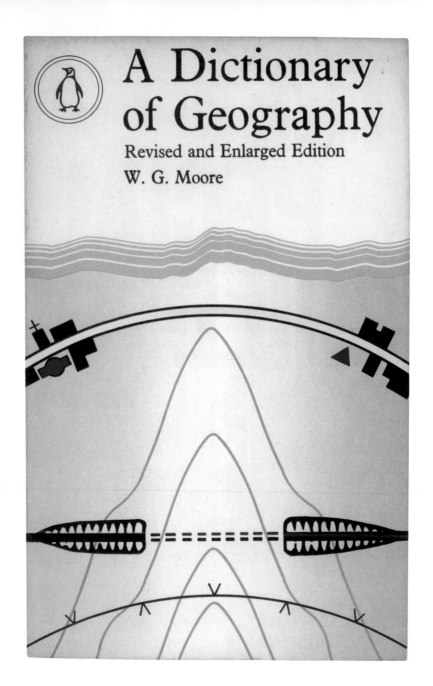

A Dictionary
of Geography

Revised and Enlarged Edition

W. G. Moore

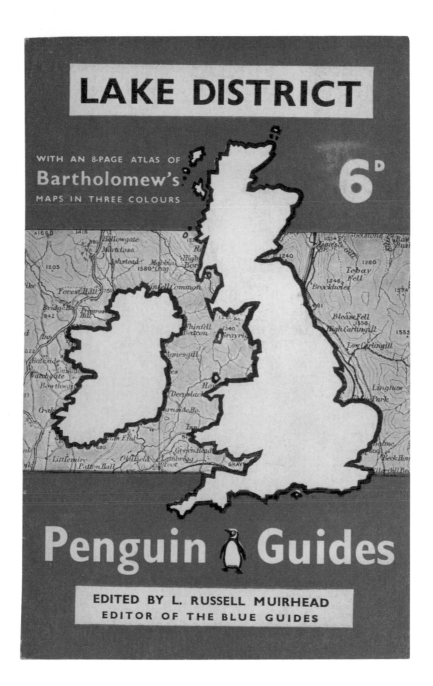

LAKE DISTRICT

WITH AN 8-PAGE ATLAS OF
Bartholomew's
MAPS IN THREE COLOURS

6ᴰ

Penguin Guides

EDITED BY L. RUSSELL MUIRHEAD
EDITOR OF THE BLUE GUIDES

PENGUIN BOOKS

Quatermass II

NIGEL KNEALE

COMPLETE 2/6 UNABRIDGED

PENGUIN
CLASSIC CRIME

EDMUND CRISPIN

FEN COUNTRY

Gervase Fen, the detective with a donnish
difference, solves many of the mysteries
in these twenty-six delightful stories

ROGER MANVELL

FILM

REVISED
AND
ENLARGED EDITION

NEW ILLUSTRATIONS

one shilling

PENGUIN ILLUSTRATED CLASSICS

GULLIVER'S TRAVELS

JONATHAN
SWIFT

Wood-engravings by Theodore Naish

HEALTH
AND
AUSTRALIAN
SOCIETY

Basil S. Hetzel

a Pelican Book   3/6

The Nature
of the Universe

Fred Hoyle

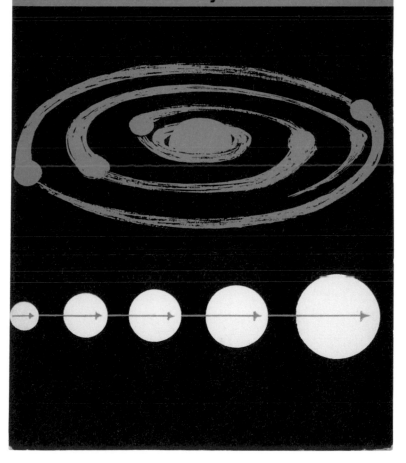

255

GEOGRAPHY OF
World Affairs

A Penguin Special by

J. P. COLE

3/6

PENGUIN MODERN ECONOMICS READINGS

EDITOR: A.A. WALTERS

BANKING
BANKING
BANKING
BANKING
BANKING
BANKING
BANKING
BANKING
MONEY & BANKING

Robert Langbaum
The Poetry of Experience
The Dramatic Monologue
in Modern Literary
Tradition

Noise

Rupert Taylor

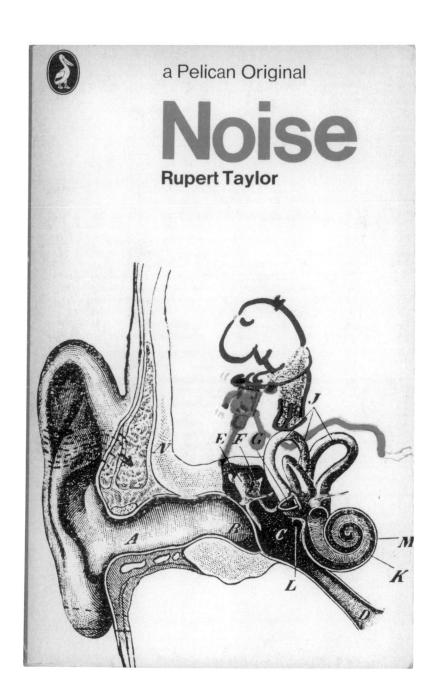

THE PENGUIN BOOK OF

HEALTH AND BEAUTY
RECIPES

OLGA GOLBÆK

2/6

an Australian Pelican Book   8/6

The Australian Ugliness

Robin Boyd

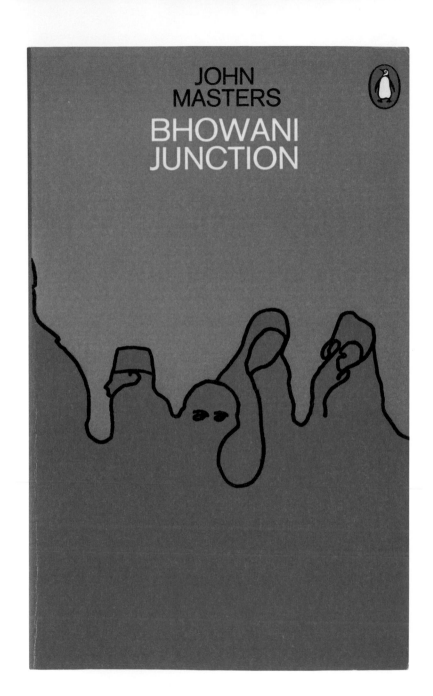

JOHN
MASTERS

BHOWANI
JUNCTION

The Kaiser
and His Times

Michael Balfour

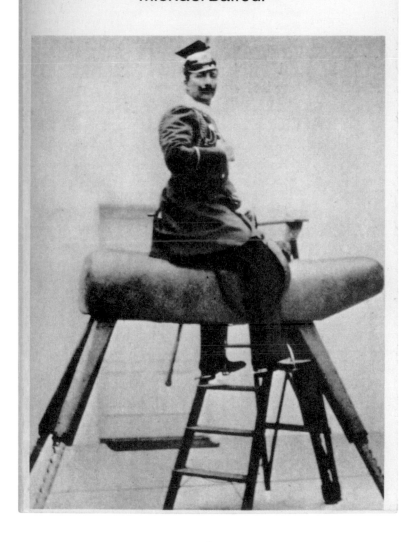

William Carlos Williams

Selected Poems

Edited and introduced by Charles Tomlinson

PELICAN BOOKS

PUBLISHED BY PENGUIN BOOKS

ONLY YESTERDAY

AN INFORMAL HISTORY OF THE 1920's IN AMERICA

IN TWO VOLUMES
(I)

F. L. ALLEN

ILLUSTRATED

COMPLETE

UNABRIDGED

One shilling and

Penguin Classics

WAR AND PEACE 1

Leo Tolstoy

PENGUIN MODERN PSYCHOLOGY READINGS

PERSONALITY

EDITORS: RICHARD S. LAZARUS AND EDWARD M. OPTON Jr

The Other America
Poverty in the United States
by Michael Harrington

The book that sparked the
War on Poverty

a Penguin Special 4/-

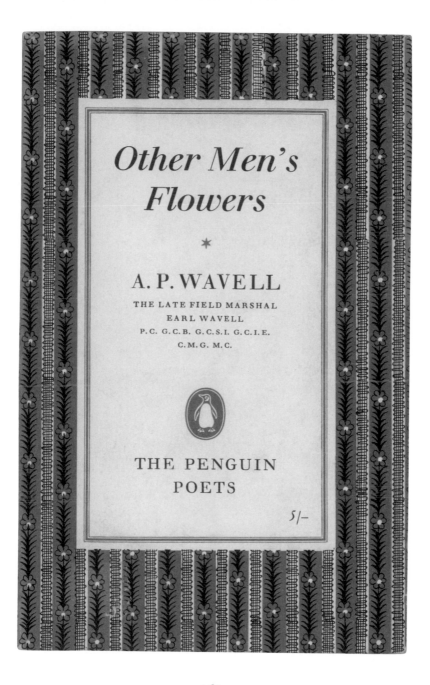

Other Men's Flowers

*

A. P. WAVELL

THE LATE FIELD MARSHAL
EARL WAVELL
P.C. G.C.B. G.C.S.I. G.C.I.E.
C.M.G. M.C.

THE PENGUIN
POETS

5/–

PENGUIN
HANDBOOKS

ALICE CRANG

Preserves
for all
Occasions

How to bottle and can fruit,
make jams, marmalades,
jellies, syrups, and wines,
with chapters on
pickling, drying fruits and
vegetables, deep freezing,
and a calendar of
preserving

2/-

PETER HEATON

Sailing

3/6

Usage
and
Abusage

Eric Partridge

Penguin
Reference
Books
7/6

TIME FOR SCHOOL

A Practical Guide for Parents of Young Children

CYNTHIA MITCHELL

A PENGUIN SPECIAL

HEALTH

OF THE

FUTURE

Gives an impression to the members
of the lay public of conditions as
they are and as some of us would
like them to be, with suggestions
of the lines along which policy
should march

by

ALECK
BOURNE

UNDERSTANDING AND HELPING THE SCHIZOPHRENIC

A guide for family and friends
SILVANO ARIETI

GEORGE MELLY
REVOLT INTO STYLE
THE POP ARTS IN BRITAIN

Edited by Valerie H. Pitt

The Penguin Dictionary of

PHYSICS

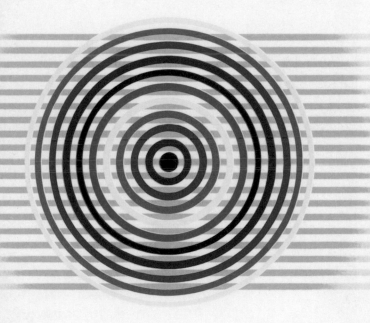

THE SPARE-TIME BOOK
a practical guide to adventure
TONY GIBSON & JACK SINGLETON

A Penguin Handbook 3/6

H. MUNRO FOX

THE
PERSONALITY
OF
ANIMALS

PELICAN   BOOKS

In Search of England

H. V. MORTON

THE CHESS MIND

GERALD ABRAHAMS

A PENGUIN HANDBOOK   5/-

Charles Rycroft

A Critical Dictionary of
PSYCHOANALYSIS

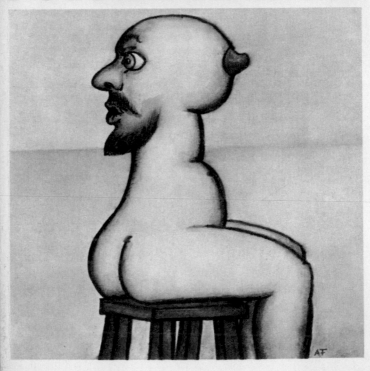

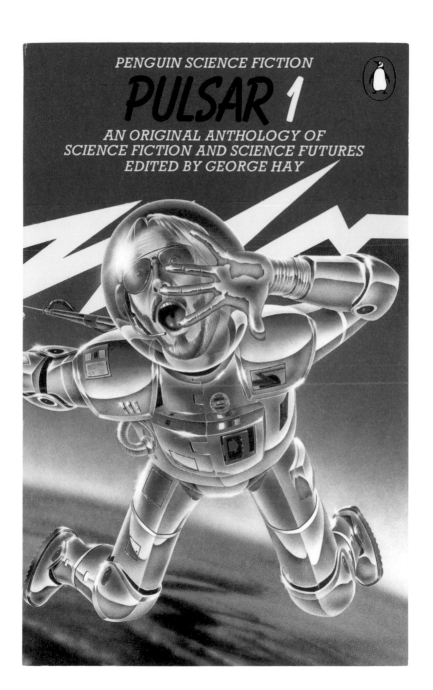

PENGUIN SCIENCE FICTION

PULSAR 1

AN ORIGINAL ANTHOLOGY OF
SCIENCE FICTION AND SCIENCE FUTURES
EDITED BY GEORGE HAY

Penguin Plays

PYGMALION

BERNARD SHAW

Illustrated by
FELIKS
TOPOLSKI

2/6

284

a Penguin Perry Mason 2/6

The case of the howling dog

Erle Stanley Gardner

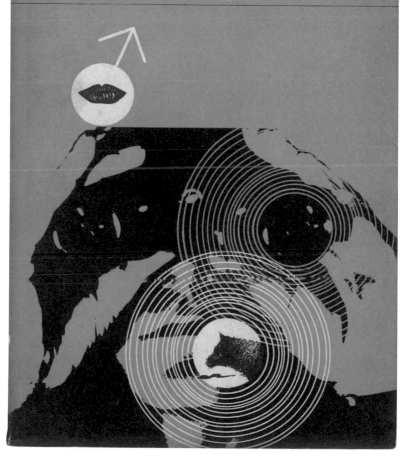

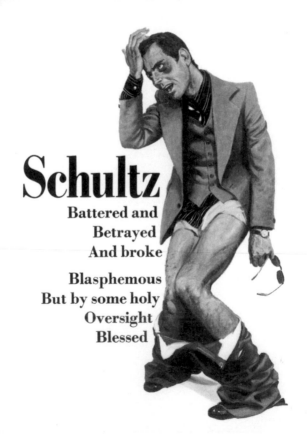

J.P. DONLEAVY

Schultz

**Battered and
Betrayed
And broke**

**Blasphemous
But by some holy
Oversight
Blessed**

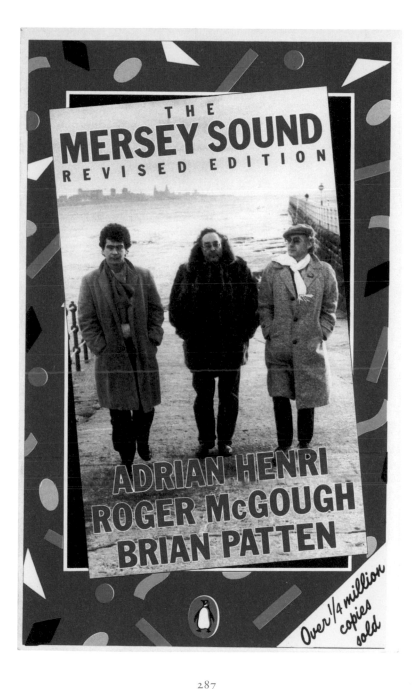

socio-
linguistics

EDITED BY

J. B. PRIDE AND
JANET HOLMES

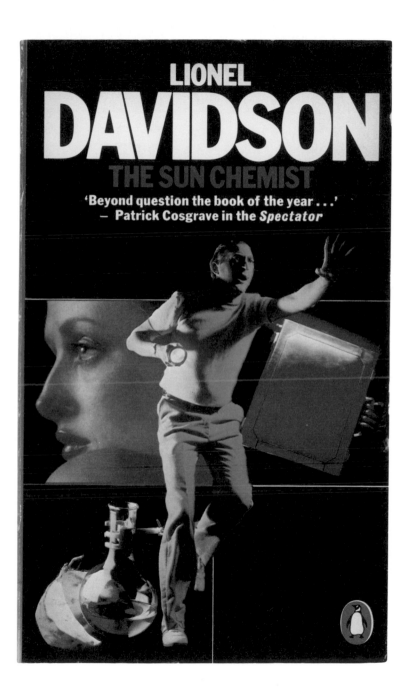

LIONEL
DAVIDSON

THE SUN CHEMIST

'Beyond question the book of the year...'
– Patrick Cosgrave in the *Spectator*

THE NEW PENGUIN

TROILUS AND CRESSIDA

Red harvest

Dashiell Hammett

ski holidays in the Alps

a Penguin Handbook
James and Jeannette Riddell

5/-

British Economic Policy Since the War

FABIAN

A Penguin Special by

ANDREW SHONFIELD

3/6

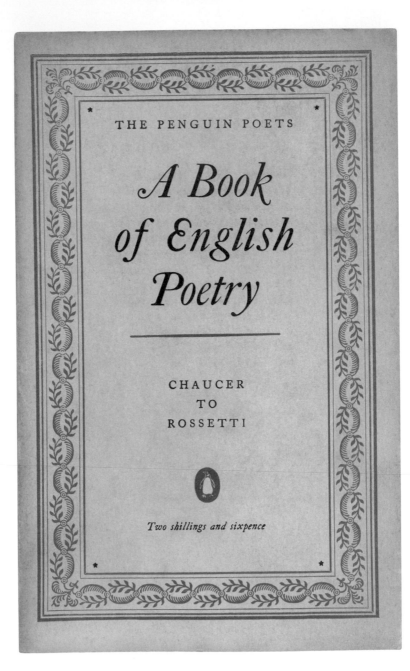

THE PENGUIN POETS

A Book
of English
Poetry

CHAUCER
TO
ROSSETTI

Two shillings and sixpence

KING PENGUIN
ELIZABETH JOLLEY
THE WELL
"Splendidly perverse...funny and poignant...Elizabeth Jolley manages to probe more deeply than ever the wellsprings of pleasure, eccentricity, and despair."
—Cleveland Plain Dealer

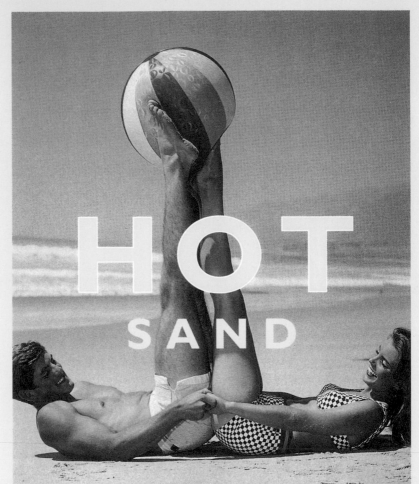

HOT SAND

Introduction by Susan Kurosawa

STORIES OF SUN, SALT AND SEX BY

Geoffrey Atherden, John Birmingham, Gabrielle Carey, Matthew Condon,

Eric Dando, Anna Maria Dell'oso, Barry Dickins, John Elder, Flacco, Jane Fraser,

Sharon Gray, Chris Gregory, Barry Humphries, Linda Jaivin, Susan Kurosawa,

Kathy Lette, Andrew McGahan, Tony McGowan, Karen McKnight, Shane Maloney,

Gaby Naher, Richard Neville, Sue-Ann Post, Peter Wilmoth, Tim Winton

PENGUIN REFERENCE BOOKS

S. HANDEL

A Dictionary of
ELECTRONICS

THIRD EDITION

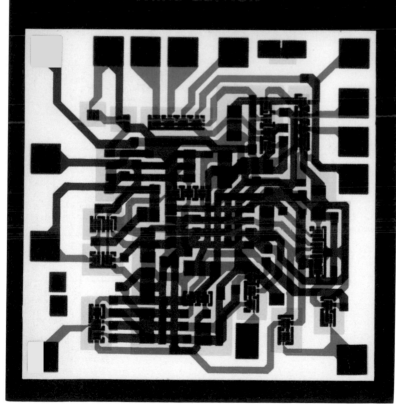

A PENGUIN SPECIAL

PAUL EINZIG

Europe in Chains

Many people are asking :

What difference would it make to me if Hitler won?

This book answers that question.

LANGUAGE AND SOCIAL CONTEXT

EDITED BY PIER PAOLO GIGLIOLI

Madame Prunier's
Fish Cook Book

4/6

a Penguin Handbook

Edited by Ambrose Heath

DRIVING MADE EASY

KEN JOLLY

MATERNAL DEPRIVATION REASSESSED

MICHAEL RUTTER

PENGUIN MODERN PSYCHOLOGY

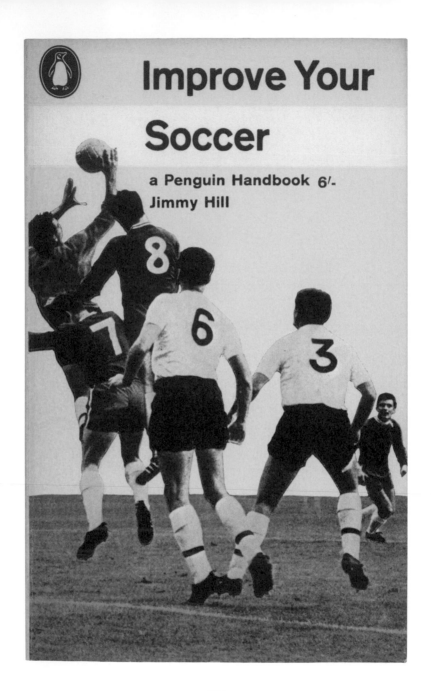

Improve Your Soccer

Soccer

a Penguin Handbook 6/-
Jimmy Hill

WILFRID BOVEY

THE
FRENCH
CANADIANS
TODAY

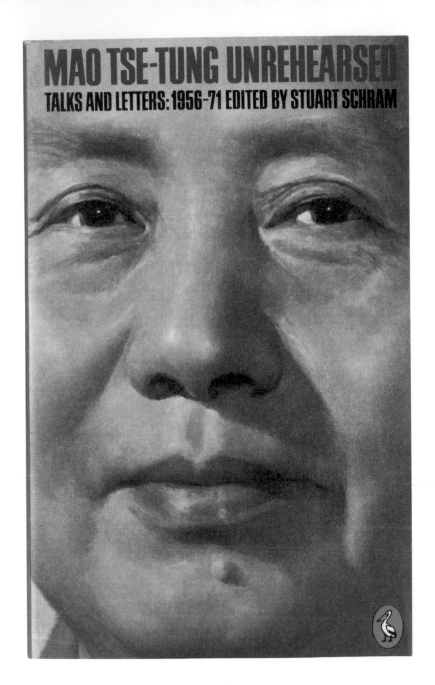

MAO TSE-TUNG UNREHEARSED

TALKS AND LETTERS: 1956-71 EDITED BY STUART SCHRAM

A Dictionary
of Science

E. B. UVAROV

D. R. CHAPMAN

TWO SHILLINGS

307

BRIDGE

K ♦

J ♥

Q ♠

Terence Reese

A PENGUIN
HANDBOOK

3/6

Marcel Hoden

A Diary of

WORLD AFFAIRS

A PENGUIN SPECIAL

a Penguin Book 3/6

No Signposts in the Sea

V. Sackville-West

The Maltese falcon

Dashiell Hammett

The Film Director as Superstar

Joseph Gelmis

Monica Dickens
No More
Meadows

THIS
SLIMMING
BUSINESS

JOHN YUDKIN

A PENGUIN HANDBOOK 3'6

Penguin Crime

2/6

Maigret and the burglar's wife

Simenon

ANNE SUMMERS

DAMNED
WHORES
AND
GOD'S POLICE

The Colonization of Women in Australia

DAVID POWNALL

THE RAINING TREE WAR

Duchess of Atholl, M.P.

SEARCHLIGHT ON SPAIN

2nd impression
within a week!

A TOTAL OF

100,000 copies

Highland Dress

—

A KING PENGUIN
BOOK

A Wine Primer

André Simon

a Pelican Book

Antibodies and Immunity

G. J. V. Nossal

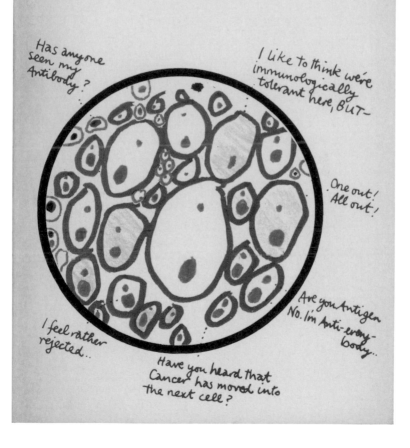

Penguin (Penguin) Classics

ARISTOTLE

ETHICS

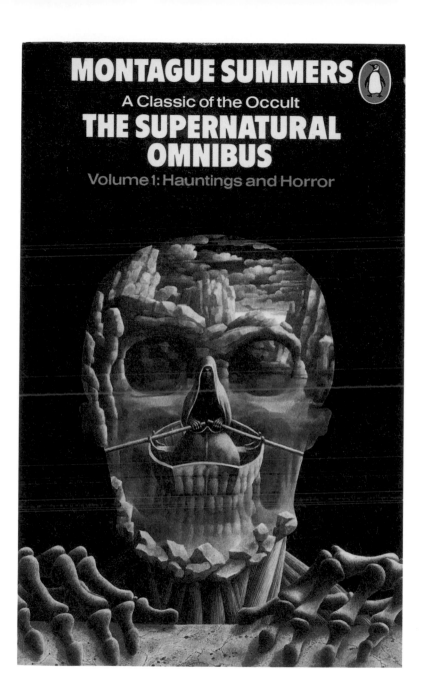

MONTAGUE SUMMERS

A Classic of the Occult

THE SUPERNATURAL OMNIBUS

Volume 1: Hauntings and Horror

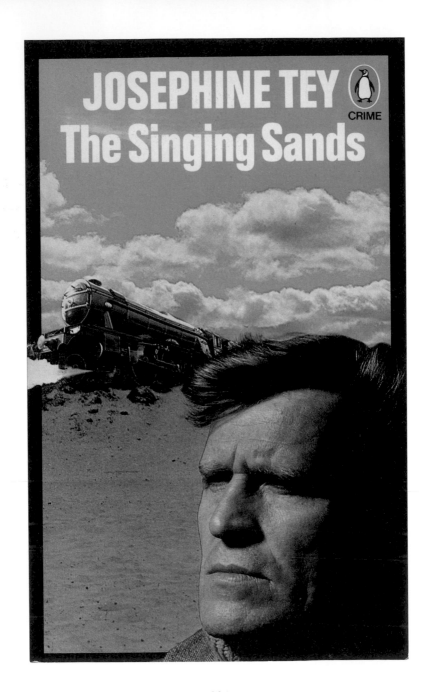

UNEMPLOYMENT

Facts, figures and possible solutions for Britain

KEVIN HAWKINS

a Penguin Book   3/6

Coming up
for Air

George Orwell

Penguin Classics

BALZAC
COUSIN BETTE

COLD WAR AND COUNTER-REVOLUTION

The Foreign Policy of John F. Kennedy

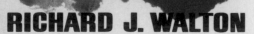

RICHARD J. WALTON

"A biting assessment"—*Publishers Weekly*

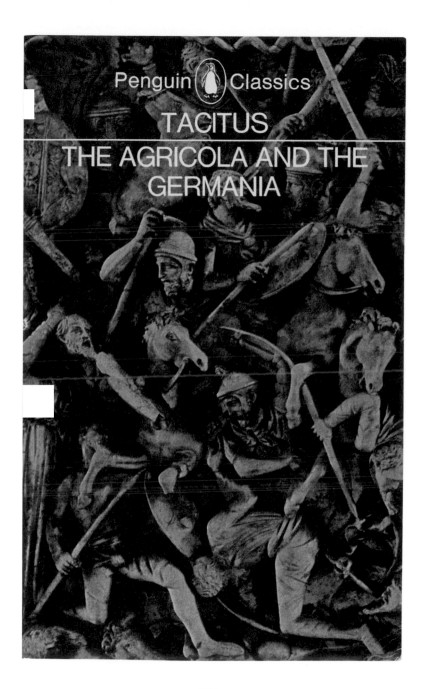

Penguin Classics

TACITUS

THE AGRICOLA AND THE GERMANIA

The Pelican Latin American Library

Francisco Julião

CAMBÃO – THE YOKE
The Hidden Face of Brazil

This book tells you how you can use your mind like a genius, like a child, a freak, an artist, by using PO to liberate your thinking instead of yes/no logic to chain it. PO solves problems in business, politics, life. PO for success!

Edward de Bono

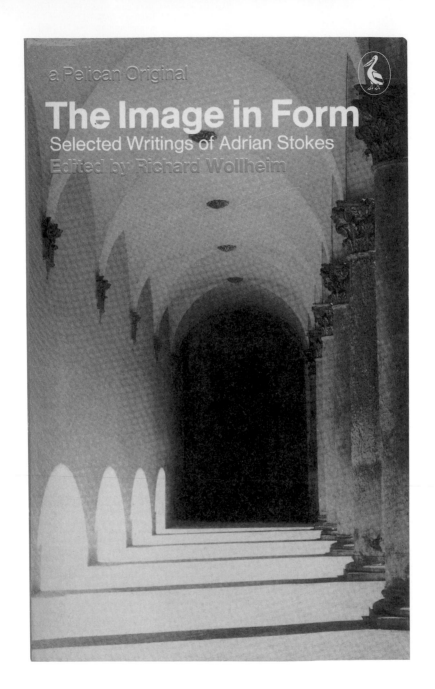

a Pelican Original

The Image in Form
Selected Writings of Adrian Stokes
Edited by Richard Wollheim

Penguin (logo) Classics 4/-

THOMAS À KEMPIS
THE IMITATION OF CHRIST

CONGO
disaster

COLIN LEGUM

A Penguin Special 2/6

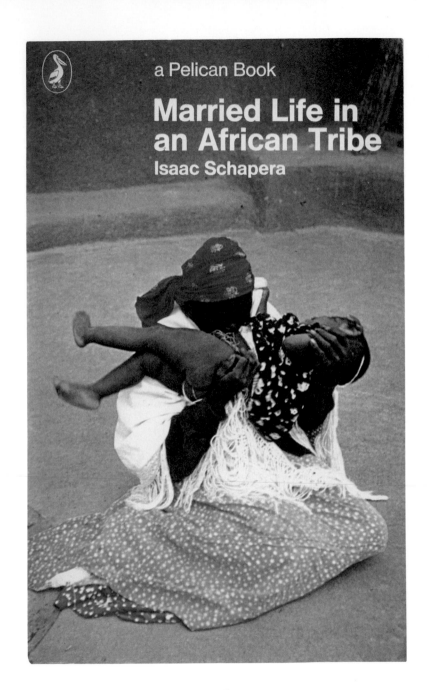

a Pelican Book

Married Life in an African Tribe

Isaac Schapera

Class in a Capitalist Society

A Study of Contemporary Britain

John Westergaard and Henrietta Resler

a Penguin Handbook

Leave it to Cook
The Slow Cooking Method
Stella Atterbury

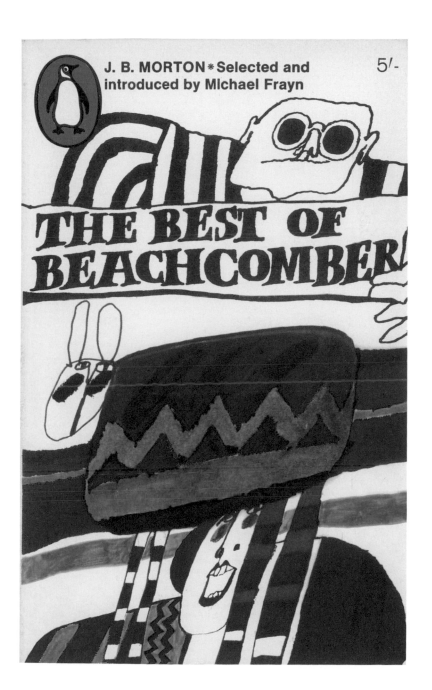

J. B. MORTON * Selected and
introduced by Michael Frayn

5/-

THE BEST OF
BEACHCOMBER

Margot Bennett · a Penguin Special

The Intelligent Woman's Guide to Atomic Radiation

3/6

Russian
Cookery

Nina Petrova
a Penguin Handbook

a Pelican Original

Design
as Art

Bruno Munari

Your
Child's Room

4/-

a Penguin Handbook
Lena Larsson

Mothers and Working Mothers

Jan Harper and Lyn Richards

Penguin Classics

LAUTRÉAMONT
MALDOROR

a Penguin Book

3/6

Wuthering Heights

Emily Brontë

Penguin Modern Classics

F. Scott Fitzgerald
The Great Gatsby

CICERO

SELECTED WORKS

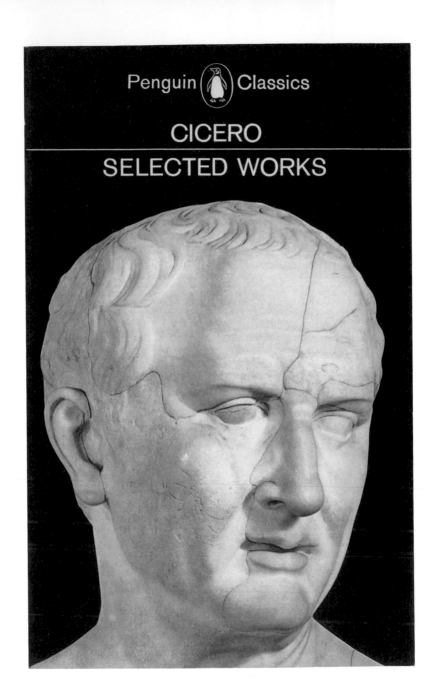

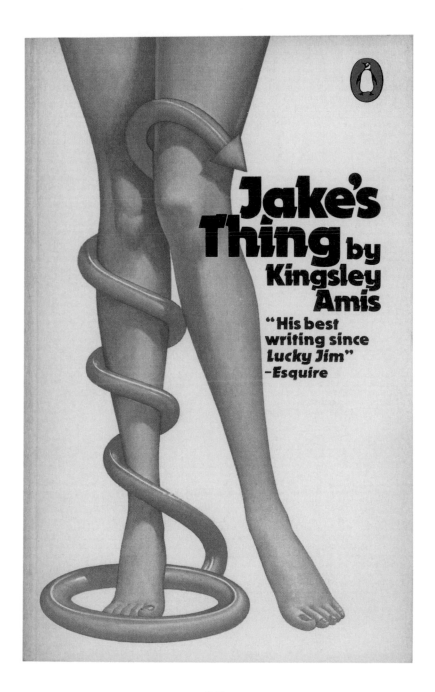

Jake's Thing by Kingsley Amis

"His best writing since Lucky Jim"
–Esquire

a Pelican Original 6/-

The Pyramids of Egypt

I. E. S. Edwards

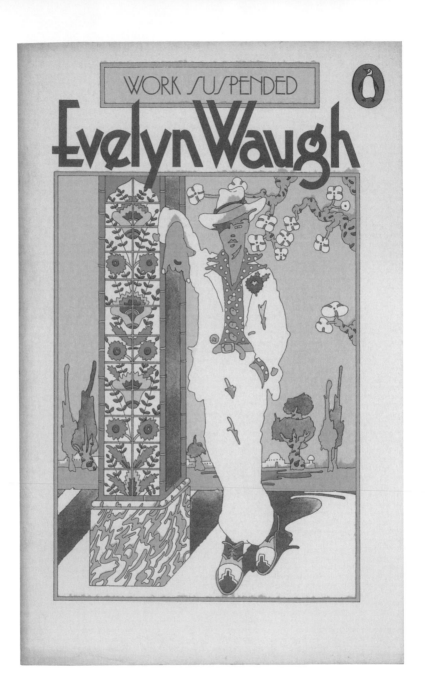

a Pelican Book

SELF-LOVE

David Cole Gordon

"A little classic"—ALAN WATTS

568

Night Flight

A NOVEL

ANTOINE DE ST.-EXUPÉRY

PENGUIN BOOKS

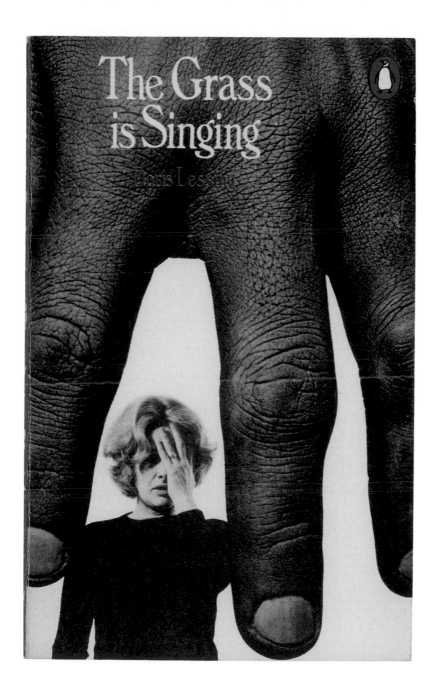

The Grass is Singing

Doris Lessing

a Pelican Book

The Biocrats
Implications of Medical Progress

Gerald Leach

a Pelican Book

The Empty Space

Peter Brook

ImproveYour Rugby

J.T. Greenwood

7/6   a Penguin Handbook

The Penguin Book
of Ballads

Edited by Geoffrey Grigson

 a Penguin Book 3/-

 Live Now, Pay Later

Jack Trevor Story

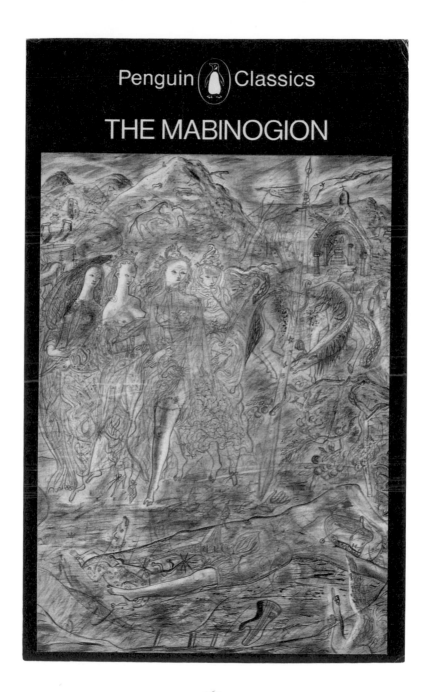

Penguin Classics

THE MABINOGION

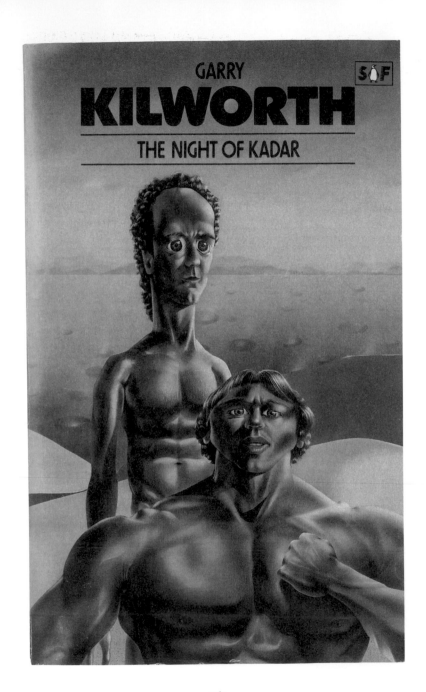

GARRY
KILWORTH

THE NIGHT OF KADAR

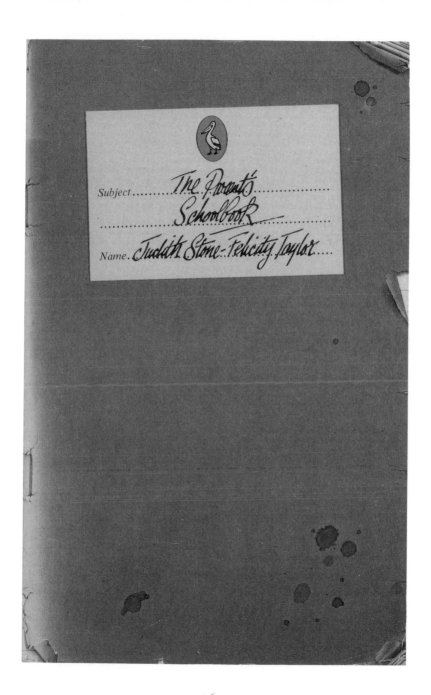

Subject .... *The Parents'* ....
.... *Schoolbook* ....

Name . *Judith Stone - Felicity Taylor* .....

Italian Fascism

Giampiero Carocci

Rich Against Poor

The Reality of Aid

C. R. Hensman

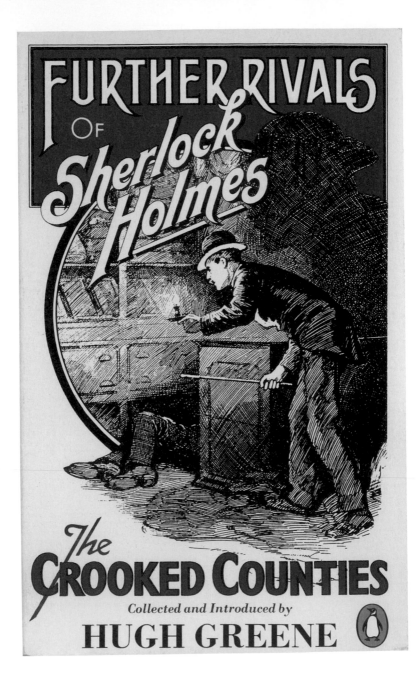

FURTHER RIVALS
OF
Sherlock Holmes

The CROOKED COUNTIES

Collected and Introduced by
HUGH GREENE

Penguin  Classics 3/6

EURIPIDES
ALCESTIS AND OTHER PLAYS

The Penguin Book of
English Romantic Verse

Edited with an introduction by David Wright

False Colours

GEORGETTE HEYER

God Is Not Yet Dead

Vítězslav Gardavsky

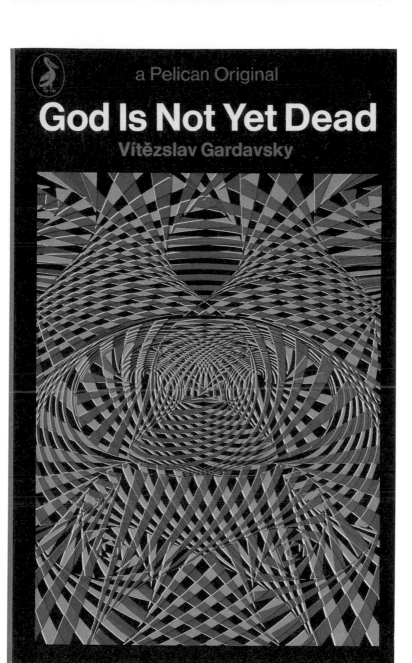

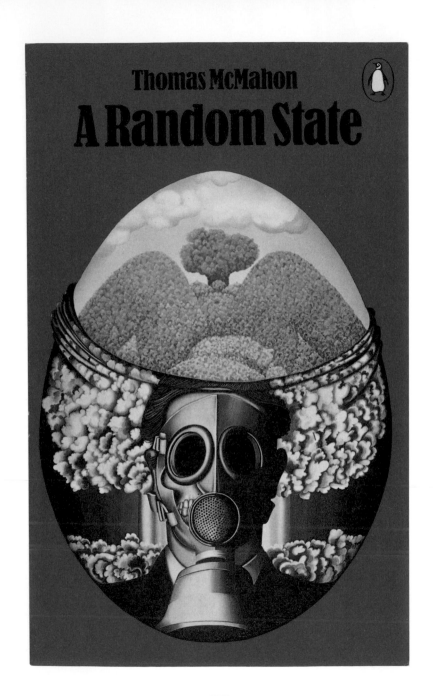

a Pelican Book

Asylums

Essays on the
Social Situation of
Mental Patients
and Other Inmates

Erving Goffman

PENGUIN BOOKS

TRAVEL AND ADVENTURE

ESCAPE TO SWITZERLAND

G. R. DE BEER, F.R.S.

TRAVEL AND ADVENTURE

SERVICES EDITION

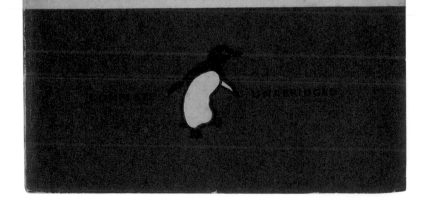

mountaineering

From Hill Walking to Alpine Climbing

a Penguin Handbook

Alan Blackshaw

Approved by the British Mountaineering
Council and the Association of
Scottish Climbing Clubs

Glass

through
the
ages

WITH 96 PLATES

E. Barrington
Haynes

A PELICAN BOOK 8/6

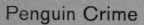

The grey flannel shroud

Henry Slesar

John Wain
The Contenders

Keith Drinkel, Jocelyne Sbath and Victor Henry
as they appear in the Granada Television Production
of John Wain's novel

Roses

F. Fairbrother

Simone de Beauvoir
The Blood of Others

5/-

The
RUNNER'S
Handbook

Bob Glover and Jack Shepherd

The classic fitness guide for beginning and intermediate runners

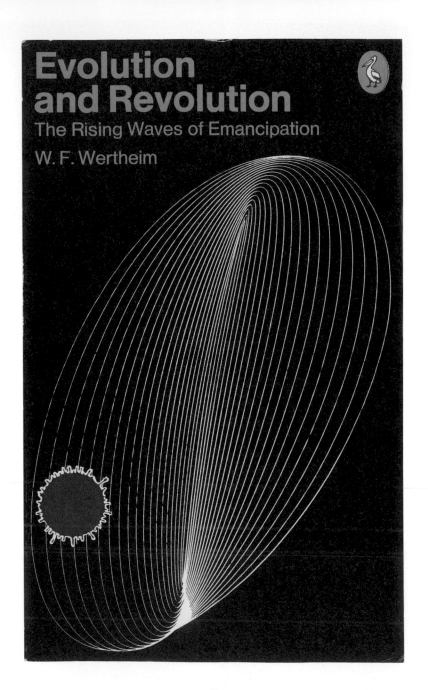

Evolution
and Revolution
The Rising Waves of Emancipation

W. F. Wertheim

QUINTESSENCE

EROTIC ADVENTURES OF FANTASY AND DESIRE

CHRISTINE
LEOV LEALAND

a Penguin Handbook 10/6

Hardy Bulbs 2

Cyril F. Coleman

prepared in collaboration with the
Royal Horticultural Society

Pelican Biographies

Roland Penrose

Picasso

His Life and Work

638

PORTRAIT OF
JENNIE

ROBERT NATHAN

jonas

complete **PENGUIN BOOKS** unabridged

581

god's little acre

**ERSKINE
CALDWELL**

jonas

13 PRINTINGS—2,873,565 COPIES

complete **PENGUIN BOOKS** unabridged

3/6 a Penguin Special

Britain in the Sixties
Housing Stanley Alderson

COLETTE

Chéri
The Last of Chéri

J. B. Whittow

Geology and Scenery in Ireland

The Pelican Latin American Library

Miguel Arraes

BRAZIL:
THE PEOPLE AND THE POWER

633

EDNA FERBER
GREAT SON

complete **PENGUIN BOOKS** unabridged

a Penguin Book 5/-

The Ambassadress

Frances Parkinson Keyes

Exist-
ential-
ism

John Macquarrie

a Pelican Book

The Great Terror

Robert Conquest

PENGUIN BOOKS

Further Fables for Our Time

James Thurber

2/6 COMPLETE · UNABRIDGED

The Loss
of El Dorado
V. S. Naipaul

NORMAN LEWIS

THE HONOURED SOCIETY

THE MAFIA

THE POLLUTION HANDBOOK

The ACE/*Sunday Times* Clean Air and
Water Surveys

RICHARD MABEY

Penguin Books

THE APPLE CART

Bernard Shaw

50c

Jean-Paul Sartre
Nausea

TED HONDERICH
PUNISHMENT
THE SUPPOSED JUSTIFICATIONS

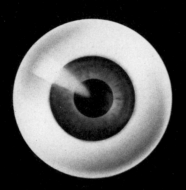

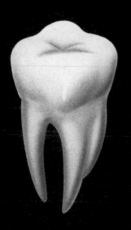

With a new Postscript

Penguin Modern Classics

**Olivia
by Olivia**

JOHN PIPER

Romney Marsh

—

A KING PENGUIN
BOOK

EDWARD DE BONO

Wordpower

a Penguin Book 2/6

physical fitness

5BX 11-minute-a-day plan for men
XBX 12-minute-a-day plan for women

A get-fit, stay-fit course for today's town-dwellers

BORIS A. KORDEMSKY

THE MOSCOW PUZZLES

MOSCOW
LENINGRAD

The Penguin
Freezer Cookbook

Helge Rubinstein and Sheila Bush

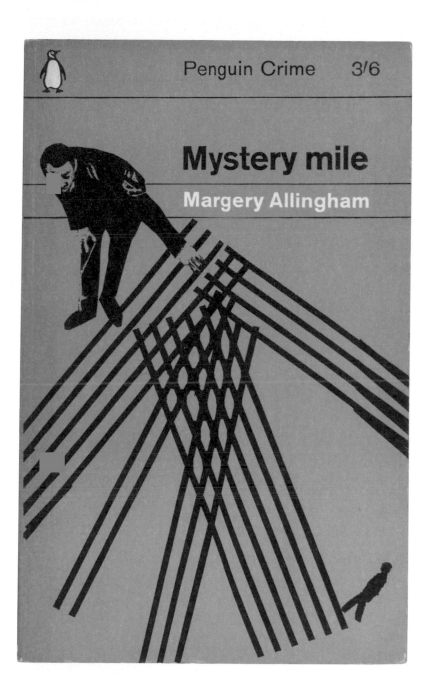

Penguin Crime 3/6

Mystery mile

Margery Allingham

I. E. S. EDWARDS

THE PYRAMIDS
OF EGYPT

A PELICAN BOOK   6/–

Too Small
for his Shoes
Laurence Payne

4/6

a Pelican Original

The Growth of Personality:

from Infancy to Old Age

Gordon R. Lowe

a Penguin Special

3|6

Britain in the Sixties

Communications

Raymond Williams

"Davies' trilogy is one of the splendid literary enterprises of the decade." – NEWSWEEK

Robertson Davies

THE MANTICORE

ROBERT GRAVES
THE SHOUT

AND OTHER
STORIES

NOW A STUNNING FILM

a Penguin Book 3/6

Wonderful Clouds

Françoise Sagan

DAVID BENEDICTUS 4/6

YOU'RE A BIG BOY NOW

now a major Seven Arts film presentation

**THE SAVAGE SEX EDUCATION
OF BERNARD CHANTICLEER**

a Pelican Original

Human Identity in the Urban Environment

Edited by Gwen Bell and Jaqueline Tyrwhitt

a Pelican Original 4'-

Sleep

Ian Oswald

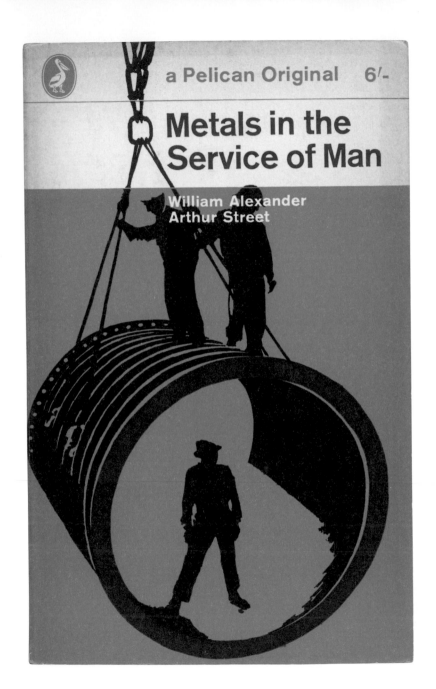

a Pelican Original 6/-

Metals in the
Service of Man

William Alexander
Arthur Street

PENGUIN MODERN POETS 23
Geoffrey Grigson
Edwin Muir
Adrian Stokes

FLIGHT TO VICTORY

**An account of the R.A.F.'s
first year of the War.**

by
RONALD WALKER

Aviation Correspondent of the "News Chronicle"

Nathanael West

Miss Lonelyhearts
and A Cool Million

PENGUIN MODERN CLASSICS   2/6

THE

PENGUIN

GUIDE TO

London

Useful Information on Hotels,
Transport, Parks, Restaurants,
Shopping, Entertainment,
Museums, Galleries, Sport.

**WITH MAPS AND
PLANS**

6/-

GRAHAM HOUGH
THE DARK SUN
A STUDY OF
D. H. LAWRENCE

A PELICAN BOOK

5/-

a Pelican Book

Beliefs in Society
The Problem of Ideology

Nigel Harris

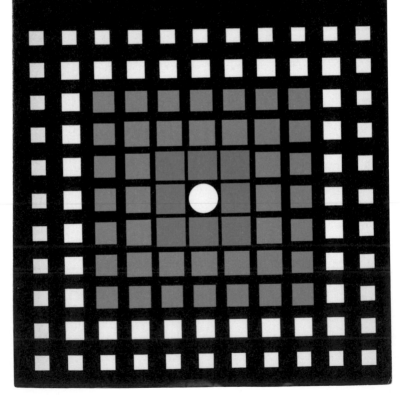

GILBERT WHITE

THE
NATURAL HISTORY OF
SELBORNE

Edited
with a Preface
and Notes

by
**JAMES
FISHER**

illustrated by
CLARE LEIGHTON

PENGUIN   **BOOKS**

Virginia Woolf
Jacob's Room

GRAHAM GREENE
THE END OF THE AFFAIR

3/6

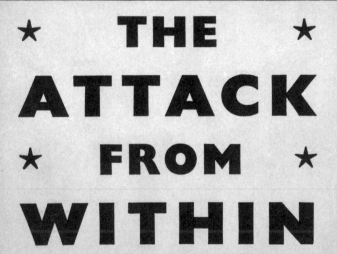

A PENGUIN SPECIAL

Elwyn Jones

AUTHOR OF
"THE BATTLE FOR PEACE"

* THE *

ATTACK

* FROM *

WITHIN

432

a Pelican Book

anxiety and neurosis

Charles Rycroft

433

PENGUIN
BOOKS

WORLD AFFAIRS

AN ENEMY
OF THE PEOPLE:
ANTISEMITISM

JAMES PARKES

WORLD AFFAIRS

GEOLOGY

IN THE SERVICE OF MAN

W. G. FEARNSIDES AND O. M. B. BULMAN

A Pelican Book 6'-

See inside

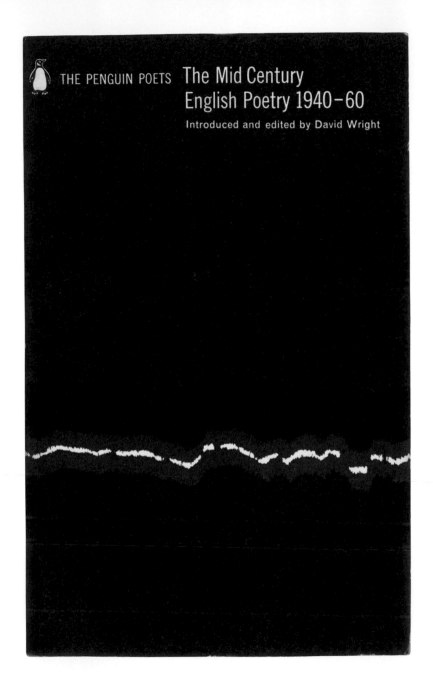

THE PENGUIN POETS The Mid Century
English Poetry 1940–60
Introduced and edited by David Wright

PENGUIN
BOOKS

ADVENTURE AND TRAVEL

JU-JU AND
JUSTICE IN
NIGERIA

FRANK HIVES and
GASCOINE LUMLEY

ADVENTURE AND TRAVEL

COMPLETE   UNABRIDGED

a Pelican Original   3/6

The Problem of Knowledge

A. J. Ayer

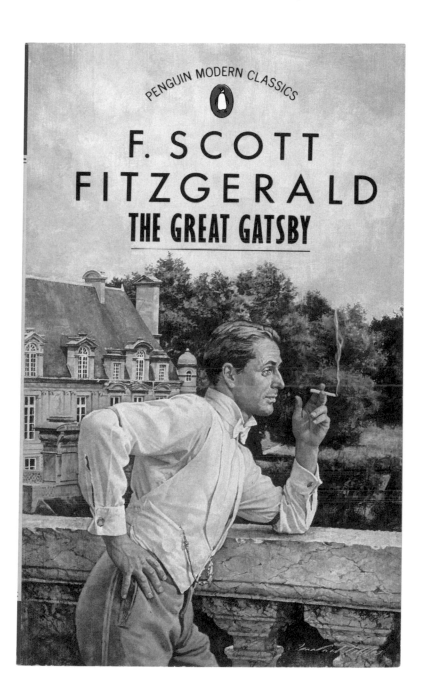

PENGUIN BOOKS

FICTION

SELF

BEVERLEY NICHOLS

FICTION

COMPLETE

UNABRIDGED

Penguin (((•))) Classics

4/-

THE CLOUD OF UNKNOWING

a Penguin Book 3/6

The Man Who Watched the Trains Go By

Georges Simenon

Penguin Modern Classics 12'6

Elias Canetti

Auto da Fé

a Penguin Book   3/6

Absolute Beginners

Colin MacInnes

MAN AND SUPERMAN

BERNARD SHAW

The Business of Management

Roger Falk

Fabian

A Pelican Book 3/6

a Penguin Book

3/6

Men Without Women

Ernest Hemingway

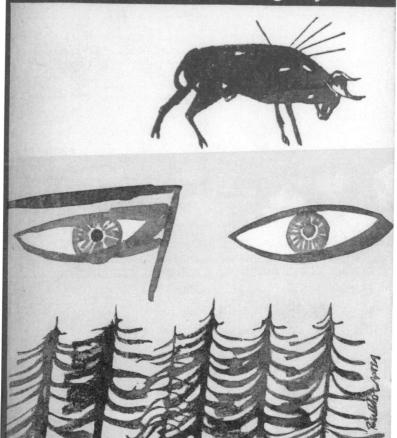

Virginia Woolf
To the Lighthouse

The Crossing of
Antarctica

Vivian Fuchs & Edmund Hillary

The Commonwealth
Trans-Antarctic Expedition

WITH 13 COLOUR AND OVER 60
BLACK-AND-WHITE PHOTOGRAPHS

Penguin Books 5/-

Edward de Bono

The Use of Lateral Thinking

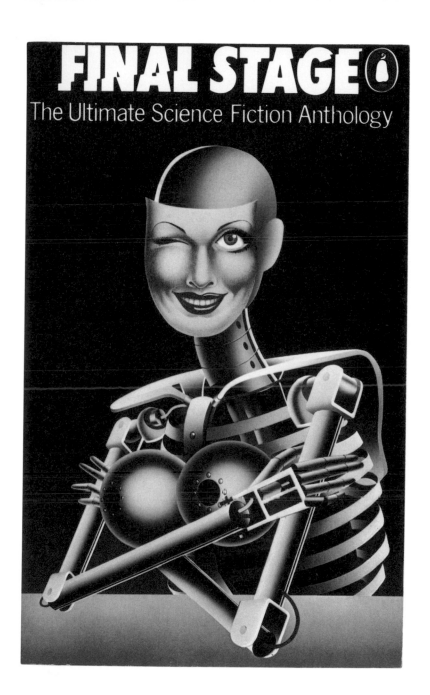

a Penguin Book 3'6

The Bell

Iris Murdoch

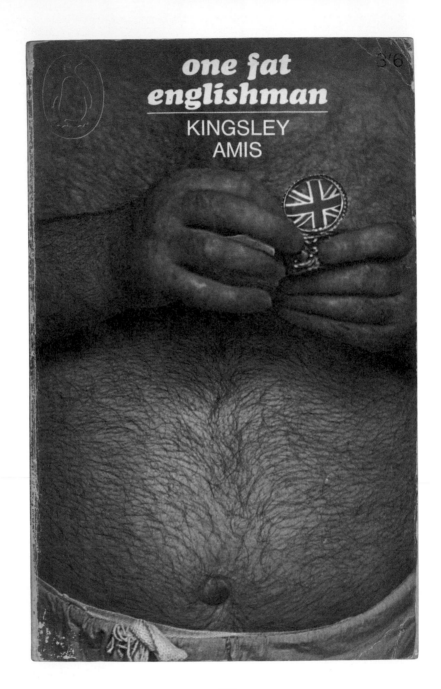

one fat englishman

KINGSLEY AMIS

a Pelican Book

10/6

The New Architecture of Europe

G. E. Kidder Smith

The Night of Wenceslas

Lionel Davidson

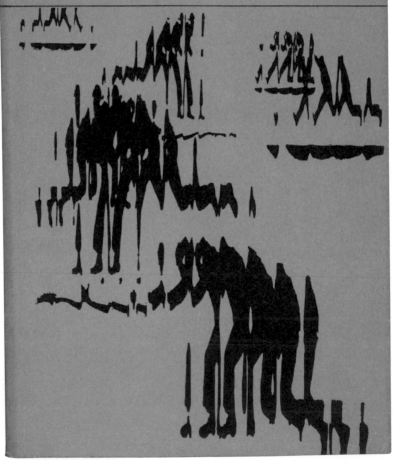

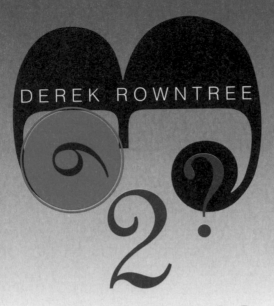

DEREK ROWNTREE

STATISTICS
WITHOUT TEARS

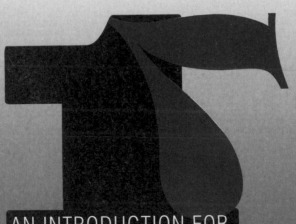

AN INTRODUCTION FOR
NON-MATHEMATICIANS

Penguin Modern Poets 24
Kenward Elmslie
Kenneth Koch
James Schuyler

a Penguin Book   3/6

the Connoisseur's Crossword Book

Edited by Alan Cash

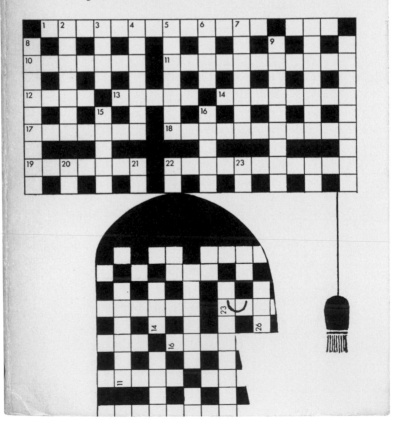

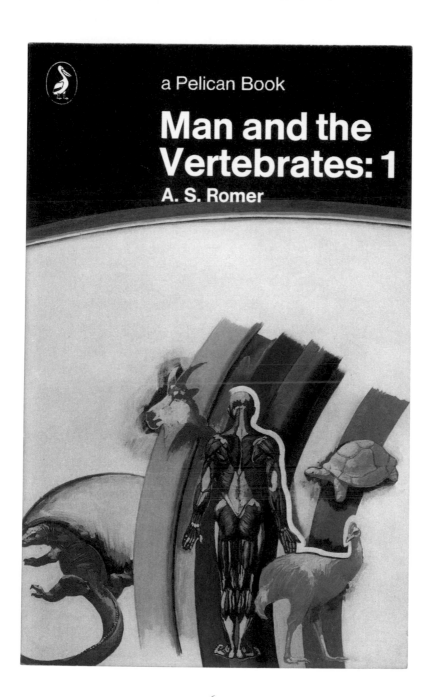

Man and the Vertebrates: 1

A. S. Romer

Carlos Marighela

FOR THE LIBERATION OF BRAZIL

PINGÜINO

NBR

ENRIQUE WERNICKE

ficcion *ficcion*

LA TIERRA DEL
BIEN-TE-VEO

LAUTARO

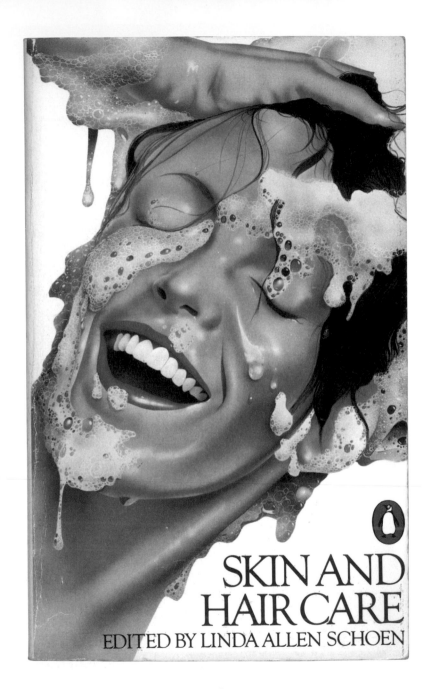

SKIN AND HAIR CARE

EDITED BY LINDA ALLEN SCHOEN

SURVIVE THE SAVAGE SEA

DOUGAL ROBERTSON

A Peregrine Book

The Concept of Mind

12'6

Gilbert Ryle

ARTHUR KOESTLER

The re-issue of his powerful, relevant and
disturbing novel of war-time Europe

ARRIVAL AND DEPARTURE

THE JAZZ SCENE

A Penguin Special

4/-

a Pelican Original

The Joyful Community

An account of the Bruderhof — a communal
movement now in its third generation

Benjamin Zablocki

"The best and most useful book on communes
that's been written."

The Last Whole Earth Catalogue

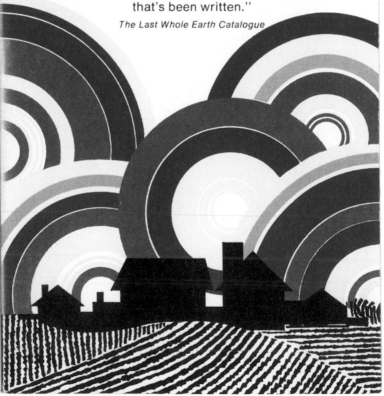

a Pelican Book   3/6

Evolution in Action

Julian Huxley

PENGUIN
BOOKS

THIS BOOK MUST NOT BE RESOLD

THE DIARY OF
A NOBODY

GEORGE GROSSMITH

AND

WEEDON GROSSMITH
SERVICES EDITION

COMPLETE   UNABRIDGED

PENGUIN MODERN POETS 22
John Fuller
Peter Levi
Adrian Mitchell

Franz Kafka

Metamorphosis
and Other Stories

GENERAL WAVELL

GENERALS

AND

GENERALSHIP

The Lees Knowles Lectures delivered at
Trinity College, Cambridge in 1939

With a foreword by

GENERAL SIR JOHN DILL

Chief of the Imperial General Staff

ADOLF HITLER

MY PART IN HIS DOWNFALL

SPIKE MILLIGAN

Instead
of Education

Ways to help people do things better

John Holt

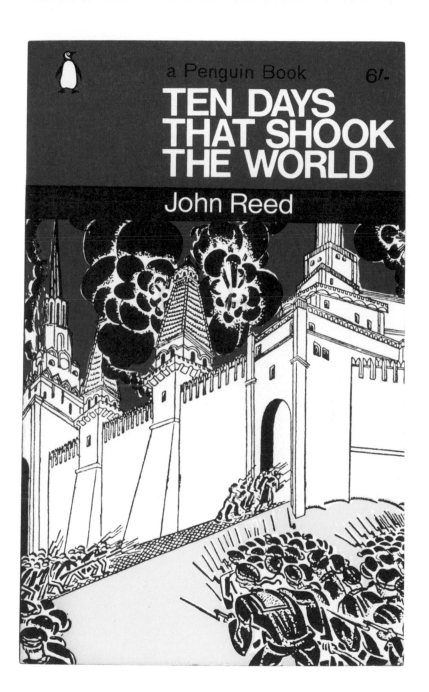

a Penguin Book

6/-

TEN DAYS THAT SHOOK THE WORLD

John Reed

The Penguin Book of
Elizabethan Verse

Introduced and edited by Edward Lucie-Smith

Colette

Ripening Seed

PENGUIN MODERN CLASSICS 2/6

JOHN MASTERS

THE DECEIVERS

David Capian

PENGUIN BOOKS 2/6

PENGUIN
BOOKS

NINETEEN
EIGHTY-FOUR

—

GEORGE ORWELL

COMPLETE   UNABRIDGED

3/6

H.G.WELLS

Selected
Short Stories

THE TIME MACHINE

THE COUNTRY OF THE BLIND

THE DIAMOND MAKER

THE STOLEN BACILLUS

THE PLATTNER STORY

and many others

Penguin
Short Stories

3/6

a Pelican Original

Literacy and Development in the West

Carlo M. Cipolla

The Reefs of Space

Frederik Pohl and
Jack Williamson

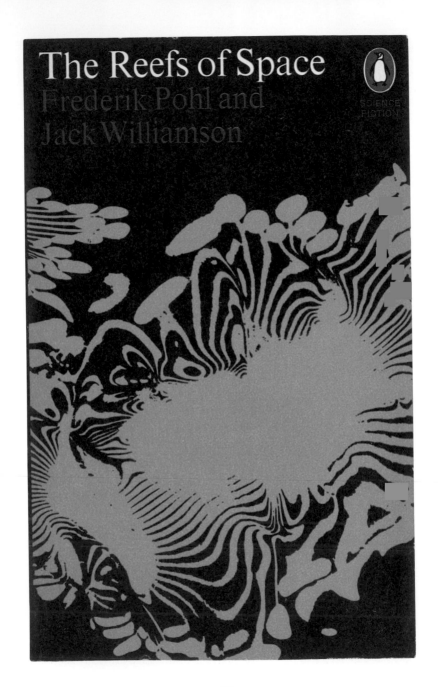

Penguin Modern Classics 3'6

Robert Graves

Goodbye to All That

Summer
Cooking

4/6

a Penguin Handbook
Elizabeth David

Penguin Crime 3/6

The case of torches

Clark Smith

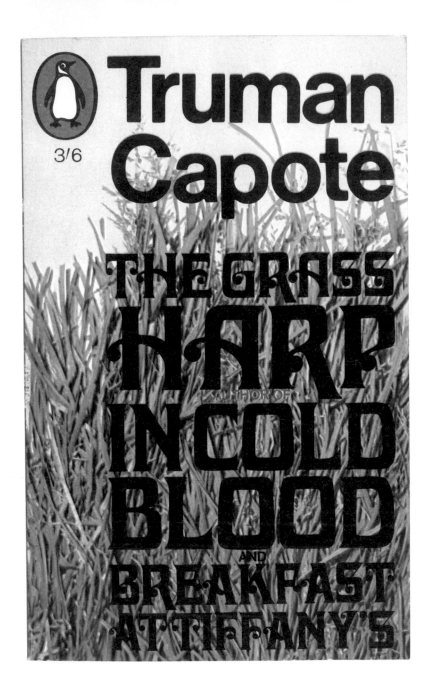

Truman Capote

3/6

THE GRASS
HARP
AUTHOR OF
IN COLD
BLOOD
AND
BREAKFAST
AT TIFFANY'S

Simenon

3/6

Stranger in the House

A
great
Simenon
becomes
a great
film

Penguin Modern Classics

Joyce Cary

Mister Johnson

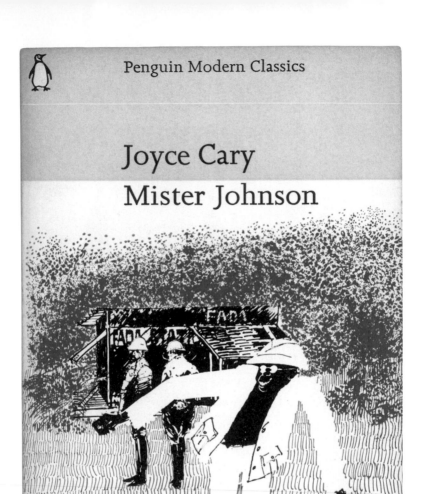

Penguin Books 3/6

ROBERT TRAVER
ANATOMY
OF A MURDER

The passions behind a
big murder trial. The
novel written by a high
court judge...filmed by
Otto Preminger.

COMPLETE   UNABRIDGED

PENGUIN MODERN SOCIOLOGY READINGS

POVERTY

EDITORS: JACK L. ROACH AND JANET K. ROACH

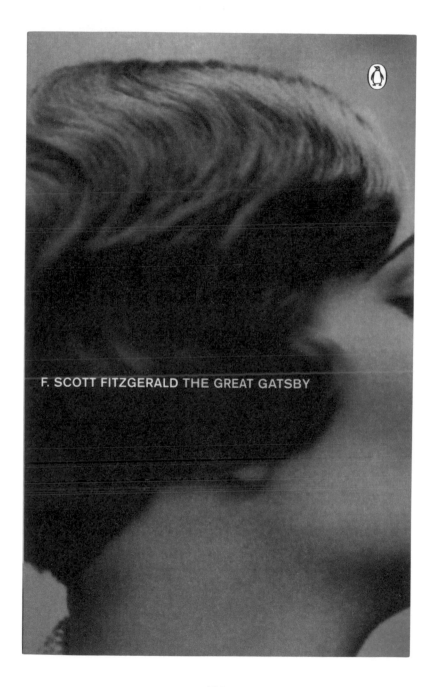

F. SCOTT FITZGERALD THE GREAT GATSBY

SWEDENBORG

HEAVEN & HELL

Emanuel Swedenborg, the great Swedish philosopher and theologian, was born in 1688. This special sixpenny edition of his best-known work is issued by Penguin Books to celebrate his

250th Anniversary

6^D

6^D

4/6 Penguin Survey of
Business and Industry 1965

The Mackerel Plaza

Peter De Vries

Our church is, I believe, the first split-level church in America. It has five rooms and two baths downstairs ... There is a small worship area at one end.

I had to call on a woman bent on visiting hospitals and organizing hymn sings among the patients, and to discourage her.

I was only always high — tailing it after everything in skirts, that's all.

There'd be little groups discussing like Kierkegaard and herb cooking and which were the places to go in the Touraine.

'Let us hope,' I prayed, 'that a kind Providence will put a speedy end to the acts of God under which we have been labouring.'

Mackerel has a long, slender face, its rather peevish constituents relieved by red cheeks and blue eyes that have often been termed 'boyish'. Round and yearning, they stand out, among the drawn intellectual's lineaments, like eggs in the wrong nest.

PENGUIN
BOOKS

A ROOM
OF
ONE'S OWN

VIRGINIA WOOLF

 COMPLETE  UNABRIDGED

NINEPENCE

W. H. Auden

*

SELECTED
BY THE AUTHOR

THE PENGUIN
POETS

3/6

understanding WEATHER

O.G. SUTTON   A PELICAN BOOK   3/6

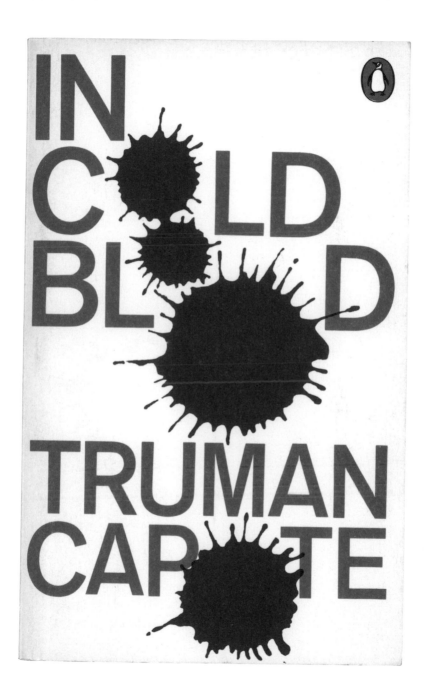

3/6

The Little Fishes
Arthur Wise

PENGUIN MODERN LINGUISTICS READINGS

INTONATION

EDITED BY DWIGHT BOLINGER

Penguin science of
behaviour

Listening and
attention
Neville Moray

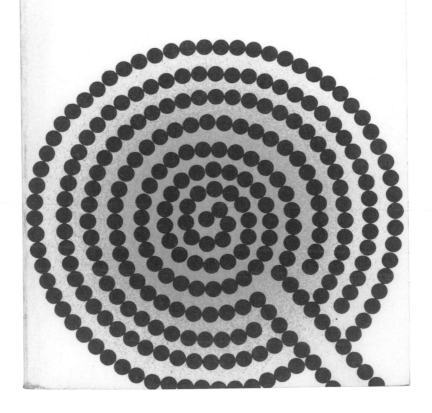

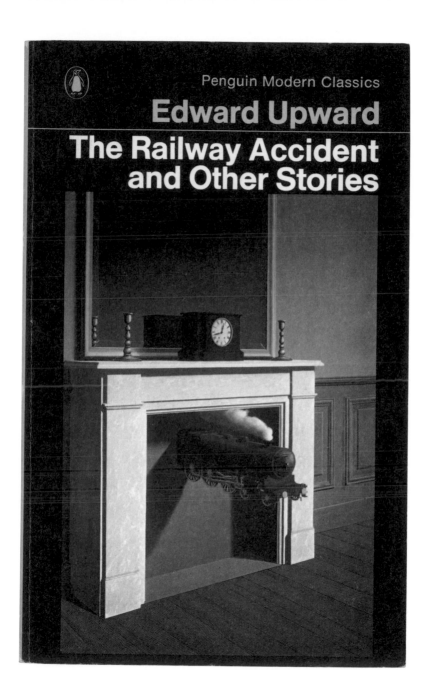

Penguin Modern Classics

Edward Upward

The Railway Accident
and Other Stories

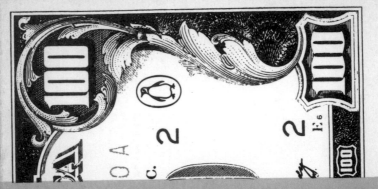

Bernard Cornfeld and IOS: an international swindle

'A splendid story quite splendidly told . . innocents and their money can still be parted on as magnificent a scale as ever before' – John Kenneth Galbraith

DO YOU SINCERELY WANT TO BE RICH ?

Charles Raw, Bruce Page, Godfrey Hodgson

THE CLOUD
OF
UNKNOWING

A NEW TRANSLATION
BY CLIFTON WOLTERS

THE PENGUIN
CLASSICS

3/6

The Penguin Book of English Verse

Edited by John Hayward

6/-

a Pelican Book

Life in a Secondary Modern School

John Partridge

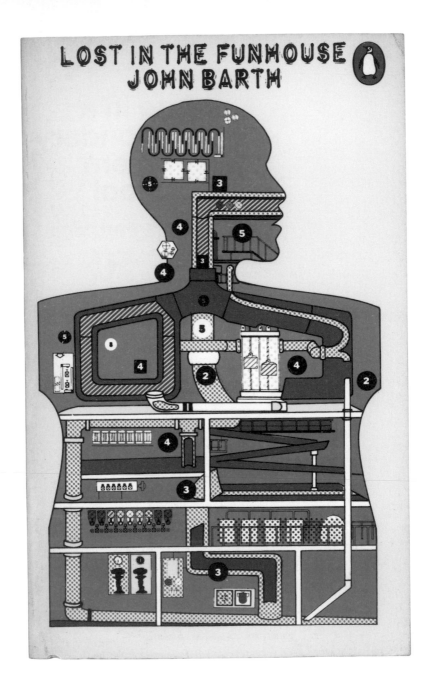

The Wapshot Chronicle

John Cheever

This day at about noon there was a cry of fire and lo the top of Mr Dexter's house was discovered to be ignited

His neighbours spoke to him with nothing more than impatience. 'Go home, Uncle Peepee, and get some clothes on,' they said

etc...

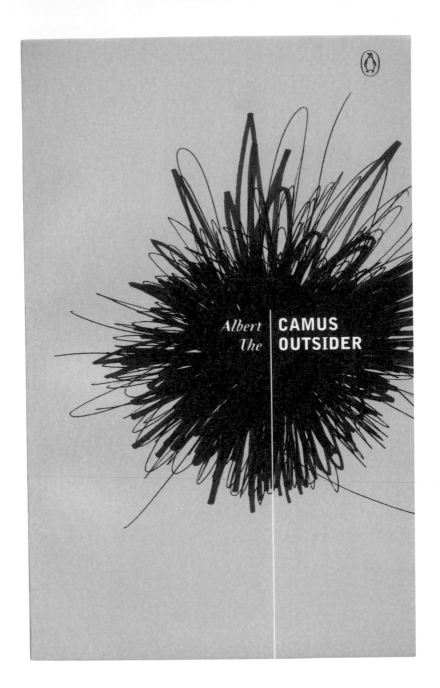

Albert *The* CAMUS OUTSIDER

PENGUIN BOOKS

THE PENGUIN PROBLEMS BOOK

W. T. WILLIAMS and G. H. SAVAGE

COMPLETE   UNABRIDGED

Penguin Modern European Poets

Yevtushenko
Selected poems

2/6

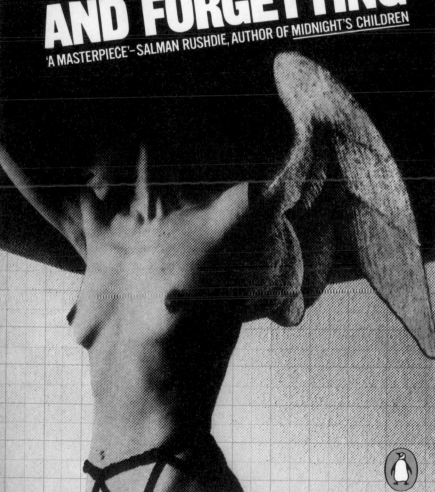

KING PENGUIN

MILAN KUNDERA

THE BOOK OF LAUGHTER AND FORGETTING

'A MASTERPIECE'–SALMAN RUSHDIE, AUTHOR OF <u>MIDNIGHT'S CHILDREN</u>

**Penguin
Science
Survey B
1966**

7/6

a Pelican Book 5/-

The Uses of Literacy

Richard Hoggart

Poem into Poem
World Poetry in Modern Verse Translation
Edited by George Steiner

Arrowsmith:Aristophanes / Logue:Neruda /
Eliot:Saint-John Perse / Spender:Lorca /
Santayana:Michelangelo / Joyce:Keller /
Rossetti:Cavalcanti / Hopkins:Horace /
Campbell:Baudelaire / Wilbur:Valéry /
Fitzgerald:Rimbaud / Pound:Sophocles /
Auden:Akhmadulina / Bowra:Akhmatova /
Moore:La Fontaine / Middleton:Celan /
Lowell:Pasternak / Hamburger:Brecht /
Swinburne:Villon / Yeats:Ronsard /

Penguin modern economics

Transport
edited by Denys Munby

The Penguin Book
of Japanese Verse

TRANSLATED
WITH AN INTRODUCTION
BY GEOFFREY BOWNAS AND
ANTHONY THWAITE

7/6

a Pelican Book   4/6

The Literary Critics

George Watson

John Dryden Thomas Ry
mer John Dennis Alexan
der Pope Joseph Addis
on Henry Fielding Samu
el Johnson William Wor
dsworth Samuel Taylor
Coleridge Charles Lamb
William Hazlitt Thomas
De Quincey Matthew Ar
nold Henry James T. S.
Eliot I. A. Richards Willi
am Empson F. R. Leavis

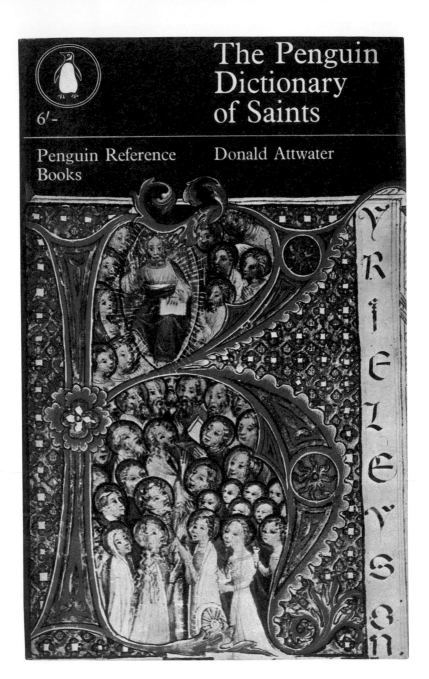

The Penguin
Dictionary
of Saints

6/-

Penguin Reference Books

Donald Attwater

ARTHUR KOESTLER

LE ZÉRO
ET L'INFINI

ÉDITIONS PENGUIN

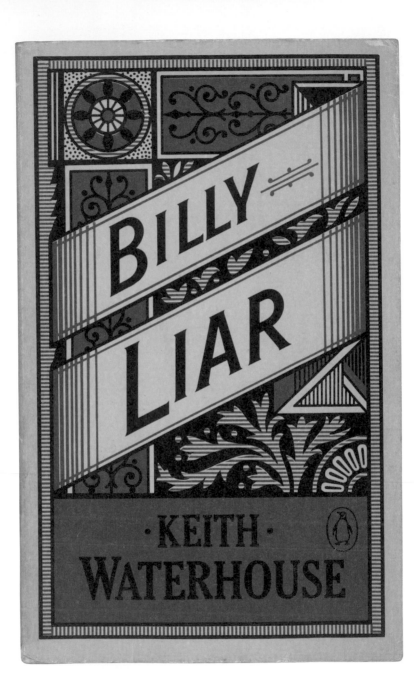

BILLY
LIAR

·KEITH·
WATERHOUSE

New Penguin Shakespeare

All's Well That Ends Well

a Pelican Original

Otto Lowenstein

The Senses

Penguin Crime
3/6

Landscape
with dead dons

Robert Robinson

PUBLISHED BY PENGUIN BOOKS

A BOOK OF ENGLISH POETRY

CHAUCER to ROSSETTI

COLLECTED AND EDITED BY

G. B. HARRISON

A NEW
ANTHOLOGY

SPECIALLY
SELECTED

ANOTHER
INDIA

An anthology of contemporary Indian fiction and poetry

SELECTED & EDITED BY
NISSIM EZEKIEL
&
MEENAKSHI MUKHERJEE

Goodbye to All That
Robert Graves

'His wonderful autobiography'
Jeremy Paxman, Daily Mail

a Penguin Book   4/-

To Kill a Mockingbird

Harper Lee

Pulitzer Prize winner as 1960's best novel. 82 weeks in U.S.A. best-seller list. Over 5,000,000 (five million) copies sold!

There's been nothing like this book since 'Gone with the Wind'

THE
KORAN

A NEW TRANSLATION BY
N. J. DAWOOD

THE PENGUIN
CLASSICS

5/-

a Pelican Original 3/6

A Guide to English Schools

Tyrrell Burgess

PEOPLE and EDUCATION, THE LAW
THE EDUCATION ACT 1944
WHAT THE ACT DID
elementary and secondary education
The MINISTRY OF EDUCATION
MIXED SCHOOLS LOCAL EDUCATION AUTHORITY
CIVIL SERVANTS DUTIES, POWER, COMMITTEE
THE MINSTER COURTS SCHOOLS SHAPES and SIZES
SCHOOL HOUSES & PREFECTS
TEACHERS SALARIES
infant, JUNIOR, ALL-AGE SCHOOLS
UNIVERSITY DEGREE 11 PLUS

a Penguin Book   3/6

Brief Candles

Aldous Huxley

The Common Pursuit

F. R. Leavis

A Peregrine Book

10/6

READING, HOW TO. HERBERT KOHL

'NO ONE NEED WRITE ANY MORE BOOKS ABOUT READING.' JOHN HOLT

Foundations
of law

Monopolies and
restrictive practices

Valentine Korah

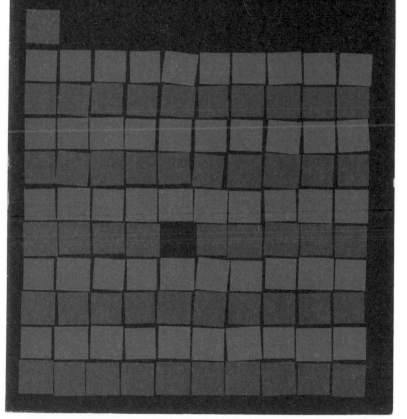

 a Pelican Original 7/6

William Morris
Selected Writings and Designs
Edited by Asa Briggs

PENGUIN MODERN POETS 20

John Heath-Stubbs F.T.Prince Stephen Spender

PENGUIN BOOKS

The Rains Came

LOUIS
BROMFIELD

COMPLETE **5/-** UNABRIDGED

a Pelican Book

Hitler

a study in tyranny

Alan Bullock

THE PANĆATANTRA

Viṣṇu Śarma

PENGUIN
CLASSIC CRIME

A PUZZLE FOR
Pilgrims

*It was an everyday case of death, sex, blackmail
and more death*

PATRICK QUENTIN

3/6

The innocence of Father Brown

G. K. Chesterton

Penguin Crime 3/6

The glass village

Ellery Queen

SOCIALIZATION

KURT DANZIGER

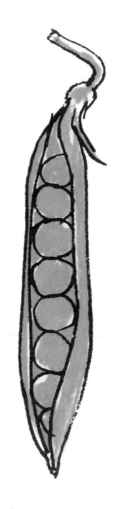

a Pelican Book

Only One Earth
The Care and Maintenance of a Small Planet
Barbara Ward and René Dubos

a Penguin Book 3'-

A High-Pitched Buzz

Roger Longrigg

Penguin modern sociology Readings

Industrial man
edited by Tom Burns

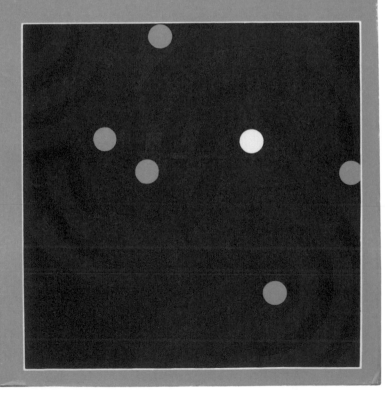

my
œdipus complex
& other stories
frank o'connor

penguin modern playwrights · 2
DAVID PINNER 4/6

Pelican Library of Business and Management

The Management of Government

John Garrett

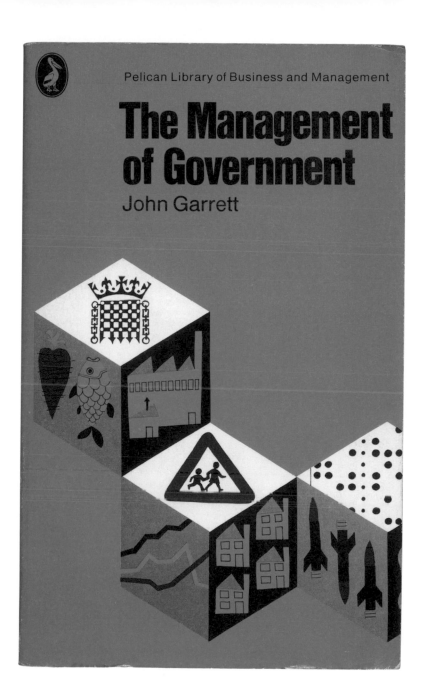

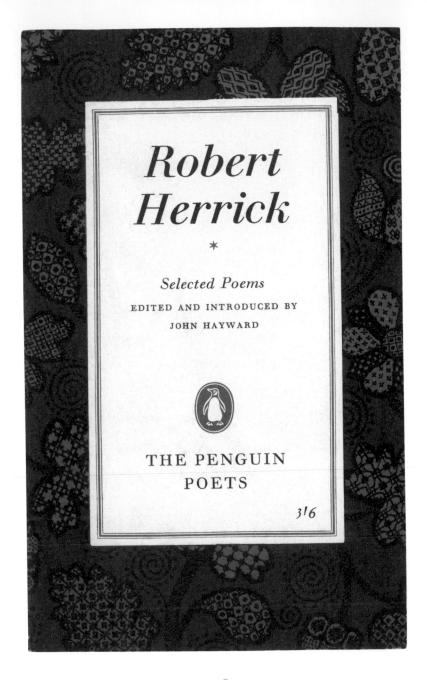

Robert Herrick

✳

Selected Poems

EDITED AND INTRODUCED BY

JOHN HAYWARD

THE PENGUIN

POETS

3/6

Browning

A selection by W. E. Williams

The Penguin Book of
English Verse
Edited by John Hayward

Samuel Taylor
Coleridge

*

A SELECTION OF HIS
POEMS AND PROSE BY
KATHLEEN RAINE

THE PENGUIN
POETS

3/6

MICHAEL INNES
AN AWKWARD LIE

A SIR JOHN APPLEBY
MYSTERY

SPIN
AND OTHER TURNS

INDIAN CRICKET'S
COMING OF AGE

RAMACHANDRA
GUHA

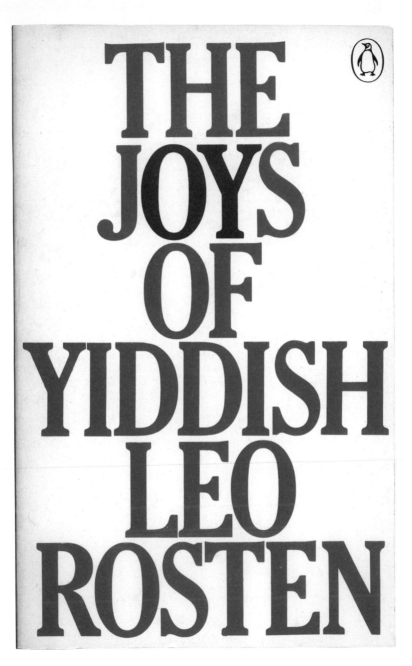

THE JOYS OF YIDDISH LEO ROSTEN

AGATHA CHRISTIE

MURDER IS EASY

PENGUIN BOOKS 2/6

a Penguin Book 3/6

The Sandcastle

Iris Murdoch

a Pelican Book

Language, Truth and Logic

A. J. Ayer

Science Fiction

ALFRED BESTER

Tiger! Tiger!

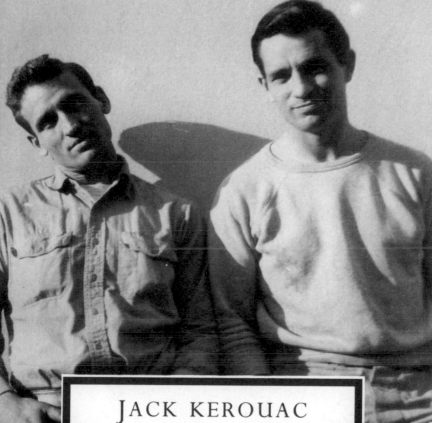

JACK KEROUAC

On the Road

The New Poetry

Selected and introduced
by A. Alvarez

PENGUIN MODERN SOCIOLOGY READINGS

ETHNOMETHODOLOGY

EDITOR: ROY TURNER

NEW BIOLOGY

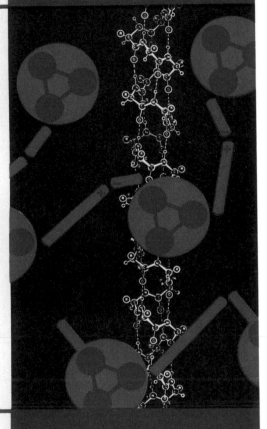

CONTENTS OF NUMBER

16

THE
ORIGIN OF
LIFE

CONTRIBUTIONS BY
J. B. S. Haldane
J. D. Bernal · N. W. Pirie
J. W. S. Pringle

—

Organisms as Physico-
Chemical Machines

Two 'Living Fossils'

Root Eelworms

The Stem Apex of a
Dicotyledon

PENGUIN BOOKS

2/-

Cyril Connolly

Enemies of Promise

PENGUIN MODERN CLASSICS 3/6

Penguin African Library

Africa in Social Change

P. C. Lloyd

Changing Traditional Societies in the Modern World

a Pelican Original

5/-

The Contemporary Cinema

Penelope Houston

CULTURE AGAINST MAN

JULES HENRY

William S.

Burroughs

Junk–

y

'A legend in his own lifetime' Will Self,
Guardian

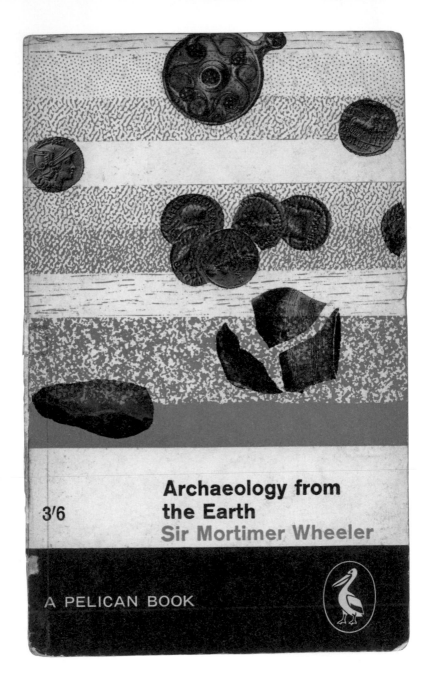

**Archaeology from
the Earth**

3/6

Sir Mortimer Wheeler

A PELICAN BOOK

a Pelican Original 5/-

The Geography of African Affairs

Paul Fordham

Penguin Modern Classics

James Joyce
Dubliners

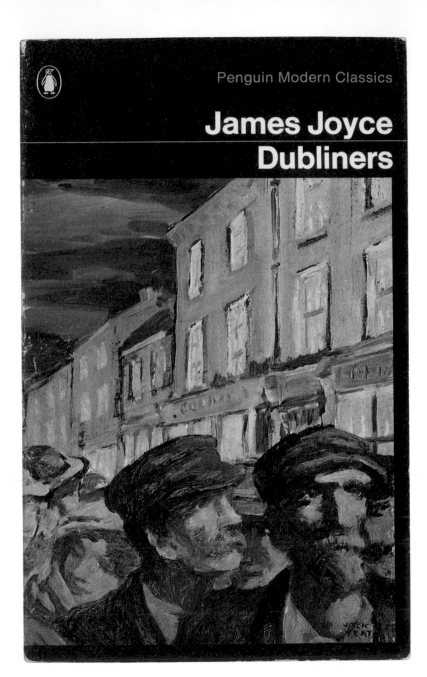

Penguin modern
management

Management and the social sciences
Tom Lupton

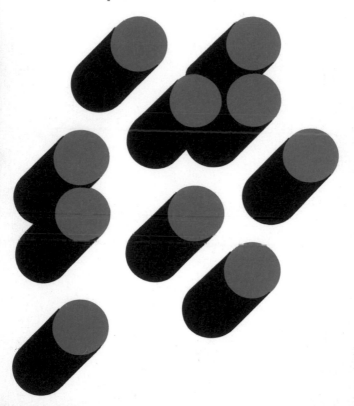

Lorca

*

SELECTED AND TRANSLATED
BY J. L. GILI

THE PENGUIN
POETS

3/6

Thomas Mann
Little Herr Friedemann and Other Stories

(M.I,N'D*
-T:H;E!
?S·T"O"P)

A brief guide to punctuation/G.V.Carey

Robert Graves
Selected by himself

A LAST RESORT?

CORPORAL PUNISHMENT IN SCHOOLS

EDITOR: PETER NEWELL

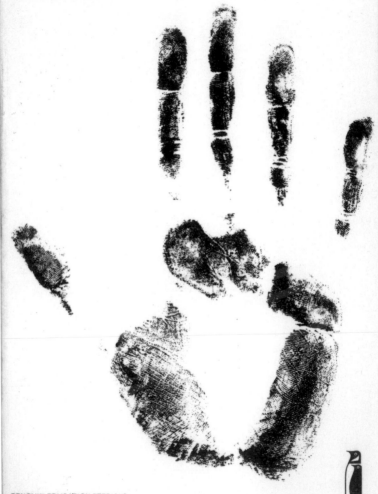

PENGUIN EDUCATION SPECIALS

a Pelican Book

Vatican Finances

Corrado Pallenberg

a Penguin Book

4/6

A Charmed Life

Mary McCarthy

HYPNOSIS
fact
and
fiction

F. L. MARCUSE

A Pelican Book   3'6

JUSTICE

ECONOMIC

EDITOR: E.S.PHELPS

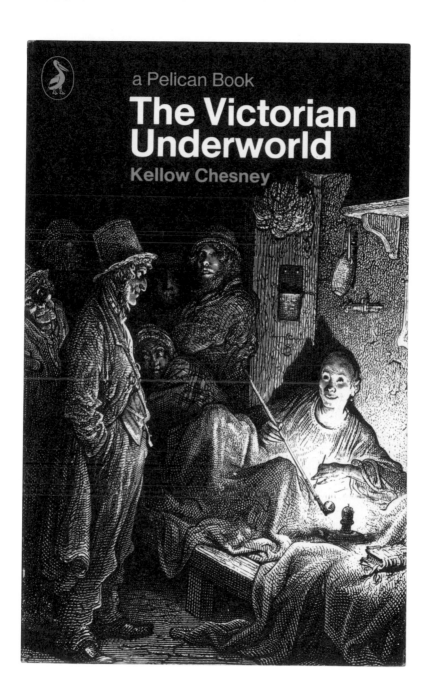

a Pelican Book

The Victorian Underworld

Kellow Chesney

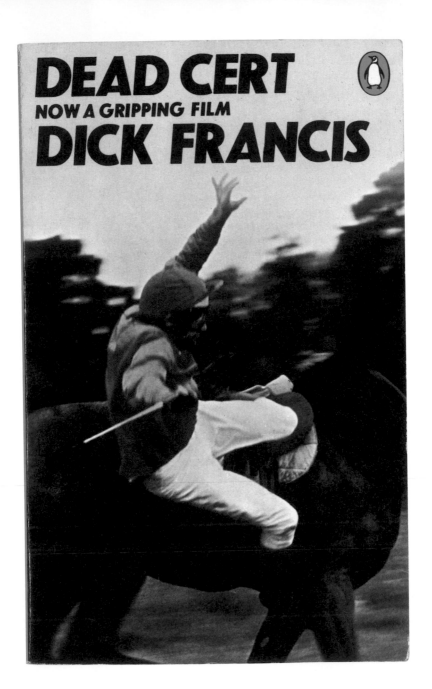

HERMIT OF PEKING

THE HIDDEN LIFE OF SIR EDMUND BACKHOUSE

HUGH TREVOR-ROPER

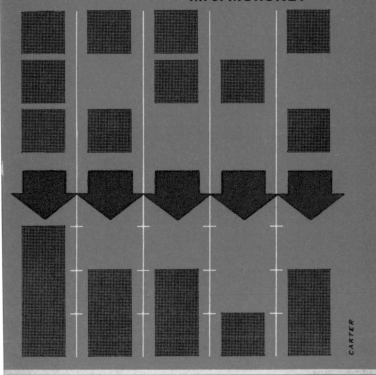

FACTS
FROM
FIGURES

M. J. MORONEY

CARTER

PENGUIN SCIENCE OF BEHAVIOUR

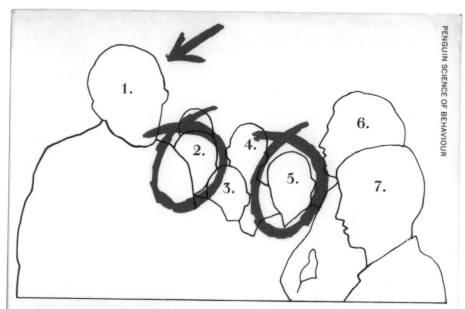

INTERPERSONAL PERCEPTION

MARK COOK

Exile and the Kingdom

CAMUS

RESISTANCE IN EUROPE: 1939-45

Edited by Stephen Hawes
and Ralph White

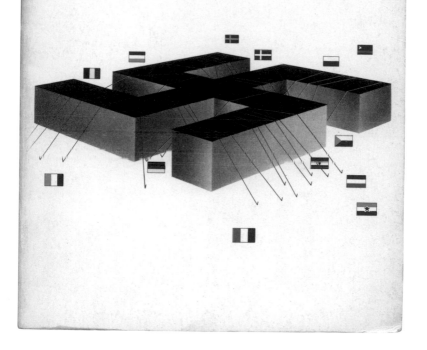

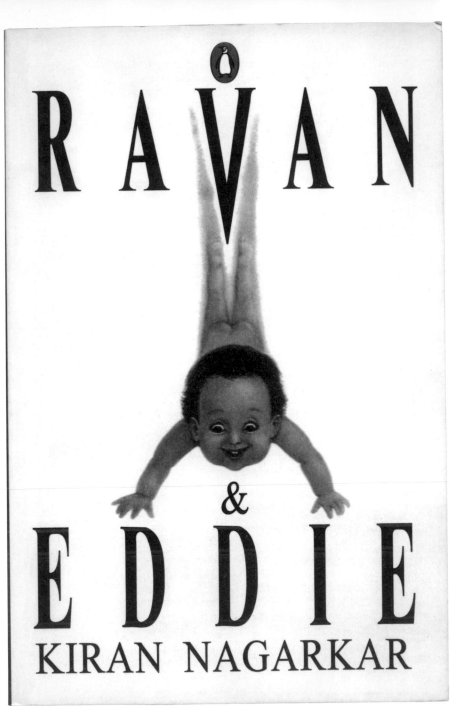

RAVAN
&
EDDIE
KIRAN NAGARKAR

a Pelican Book 3/6

The World of Odysseus

M. I. Finley

THE PENGUIN ENGLISH DICTIONARY

G. N. Garmonsway

12'6

a Penguin Perry Mason 2/6

The case of the careless kitten

Erle Stanley Gardner

Penguin (penguin) Classics

8'6

RABELAIS

GARGANTUA & PANTAGRUEL

Penguin Modern Classics

J. D. Salinger

The Catcher in the Rye

PUBLISHED BY PENGUIN BOOKS

MAN, MICROBE AND MALADY

DR. JOHN DREW

A new book specially written for this series

The
Penguin Book
of
Canadian
Verse

INTRODUCED AND EDITED BY

RALPH GUSTAFSON

3/6

3'6

a Penguin Special

Britain in the Sixties
The Other England

Geoffrey Moorhouse

This
Slimming
Business

John Yudkin

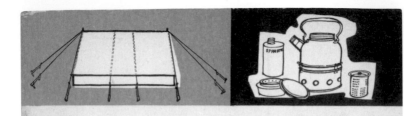

CAMPING

Rex Hazlewood and John Thurman

A Penguin Handbook 3/6

Penguin Classics

ZOLA

L'ASSOMMOIR

PENGUIN BOOKS

Elephant Bill

J.H.Williams

Complete **3/6** Unabridged

Penguin Crime 3/6

Michael Innes
**Death at
the President's
Lodging**

a Penguin Perry Mason 2/6

The case of the Golddigger's Purse

Erle Stanley Gardner

PENGUIN REFERENCE BOOKS

ANTHONY CHANDOR
WITH JOHN GRAHAM AND ROBIN WILLIAMSON

A Dictionary of
COMPUTERS

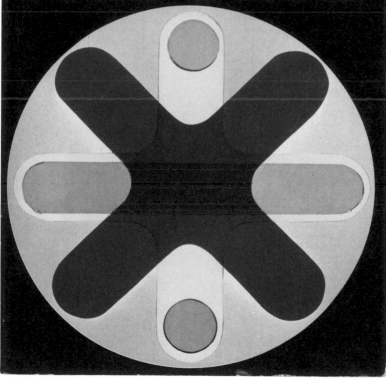

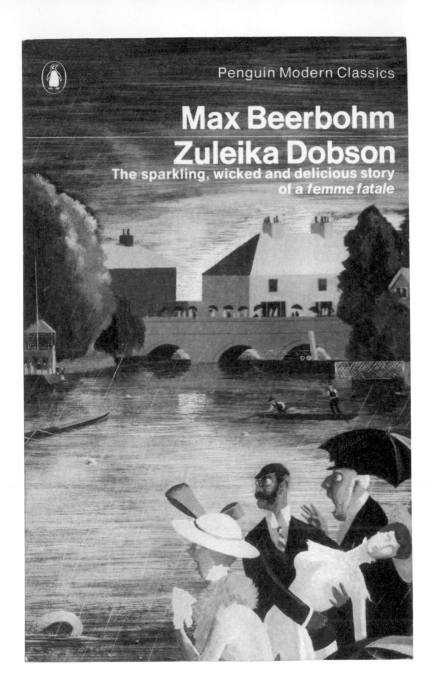

Penguin Modern Classics

Max Beerbohm
Zuleika Dobson
The sparkling, wicked and delicious story
of a *femme fatale*

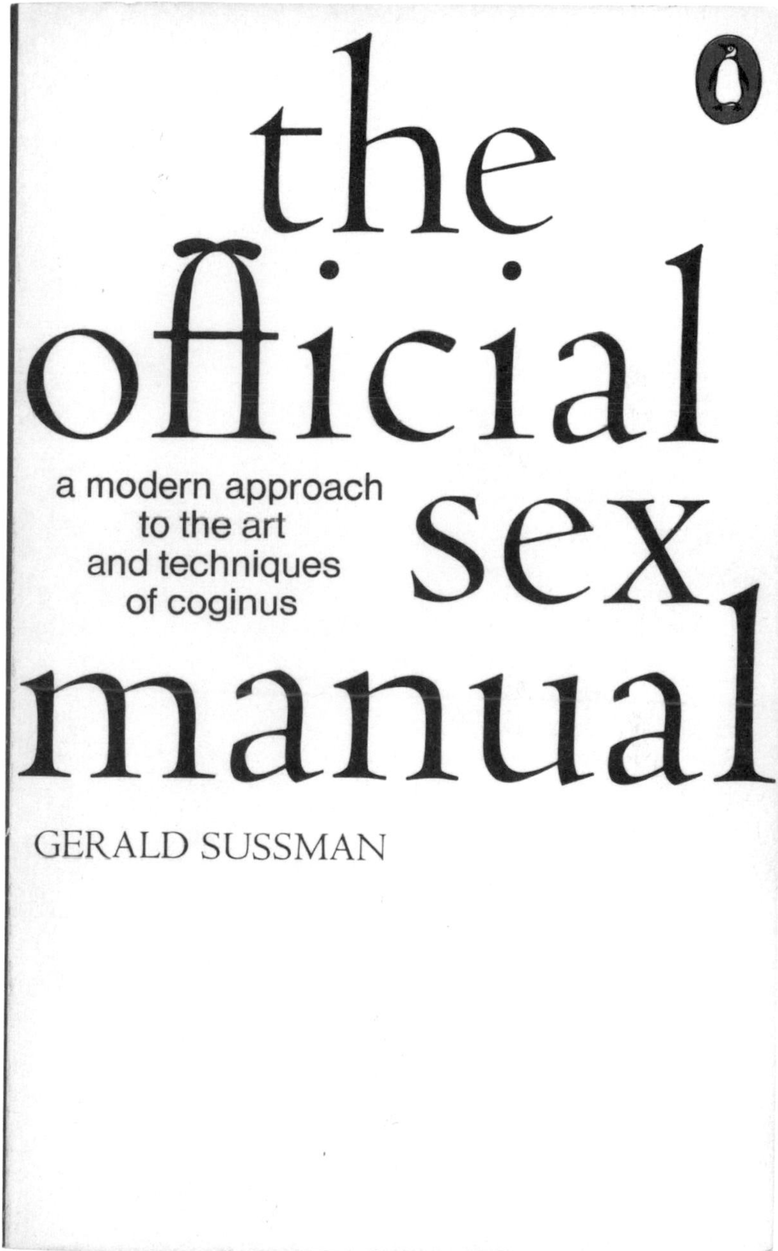

the official sex

a modern approach
to the art
and techniques
of coginus

sex

manual

GERALD SUSSMAN

SIMEON
POTTER

LANGUAGE
IN THE
MODERN
WORLD

3'6
A PELICAN BOOK

A PENGUIN SPECIAL

YOU AND THE

REFUGEE

by

Norman Angell

Two of the 900 refugees who fled from Germany to sea in the hope of finding sanctuary from torture and death. For weeks their ship wandered over the world—to Cuba, Florida, round the Gulf, back across the Atlantic, as other refugee ships have done. No refuge anywhere. At last, Britain, Belgium, and Holland offered *temporary* shelter.

With two chapters by Dorothy F. Buxton

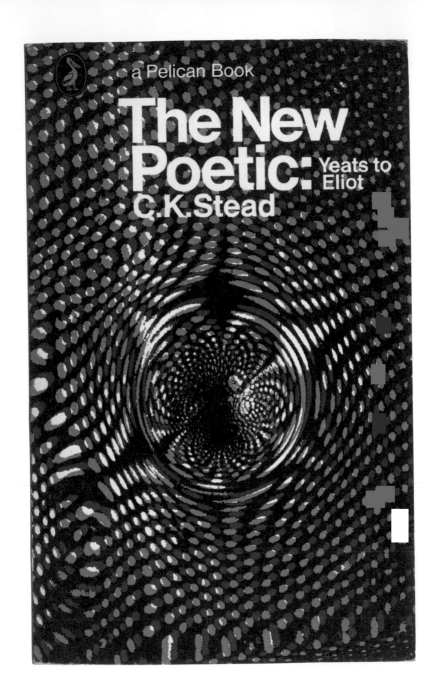

a Pelican Book

The New Poetic: Yeats to Eliot

C. K. Stead

Maigret's revolver

Simenon

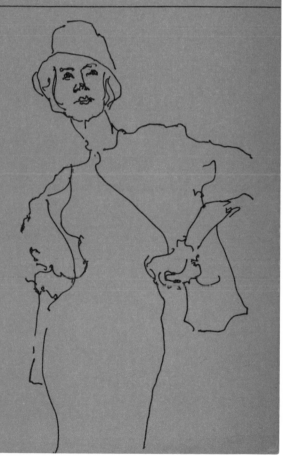

recorded
jazz:

Rex Harris
Brian Rust

a critical
guide

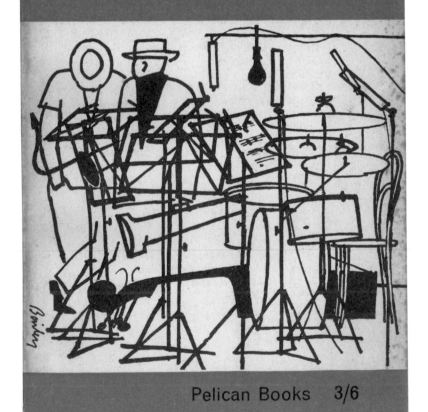

Pelican Books   3/6

A PENGUIN SPECIAL

The real cost of the War

Explains the dangers of inflation,
the difficulties of War Debts, and
the prospects of population
changes in war-time, and
discusses the question of post-
war reconstruction.

by
J. Keith Horsefield

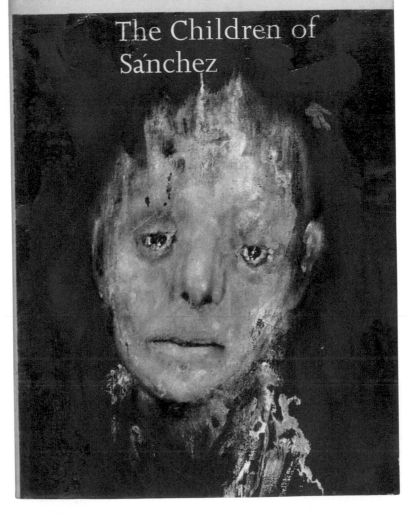

Oscar Lewis

The Children of
Sánchez

GRAHAM GREENE

The Captain
and the Enemy

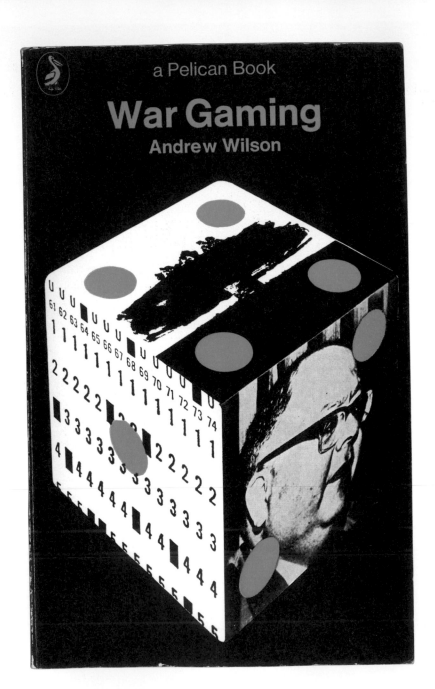

PENGUIN BOOKS

Quatermass
AND THE PIT

NIGEL KNEALE

COMPLETE **2/6** UNABRIDGED

Penguin Science Survey A
1965

7/6

a Penguin Special 3'6

What's Wrong with
BRITISH INDUSTRY?

Rex Malik

BRITISH SHIPBUILDING LEADS THE WORLD

British Achievements Speak for Britain

Penguin science of
behaviour

Disorders of memory and learning

George A. Talland

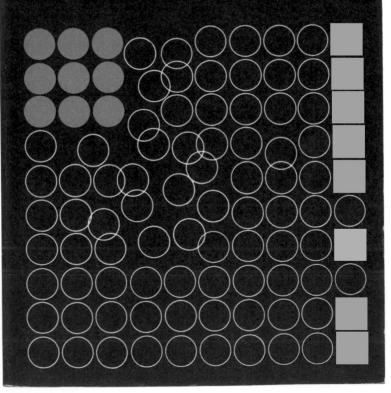

a Pelican Book 3'6

cancer

R. J. C. Harris

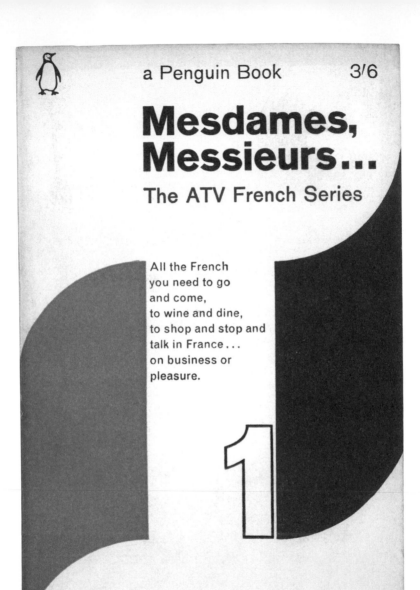

a Penguin Book 3/6

Mesdames, Messieurs...

The ATV French Series

All the French
you need to go
and come,
to wine and dine,
to shop and stop and
talk in France...
on business or
pleasure.

1

a Pelican Original 5/-

Psychiatry To-day

David Stafford-Clark

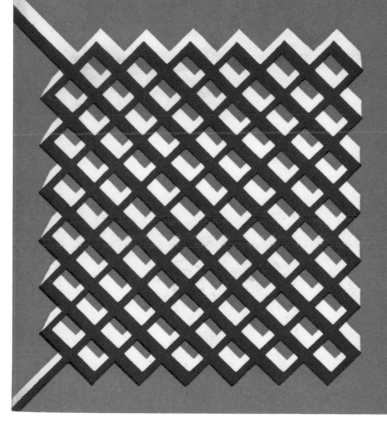

PENGUIN BOOKS

The
Go-Between

L. P. HARTLEY

COMPLETE **2/6** UNABRIDGED

PINGÜINO

JUAN B. AMBROSETTI

SUPERSTICIONES
Y LEYENDAS

Literatura

Literatura

LAUTARO

Penguin Science Survey B
1965

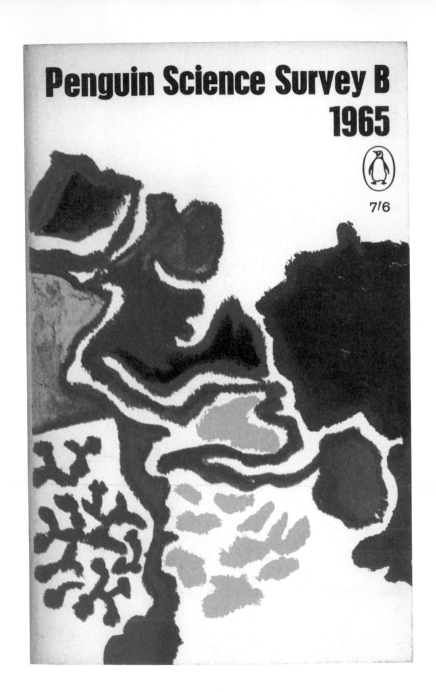

7/6

Penguin Crime 3/-

Murder in pastiche

Marion Mainwaring

a Pelican Book   8/6

The Death and Life of Great American Cities
The Failure of Town Planning
Jane Jacobs

Penguin African Library

4/6

The Rise of the South African Reich

Brian Bunting

a Penguin Book

4/6
5/6

The Stain on the Snow

Georges Simenon

PENGUIN REFERENCE BOOKS

E. B. UVAROV   D. R. CHAPMAN   ALAN ISAACS

A Dictionary of
SCIENCE

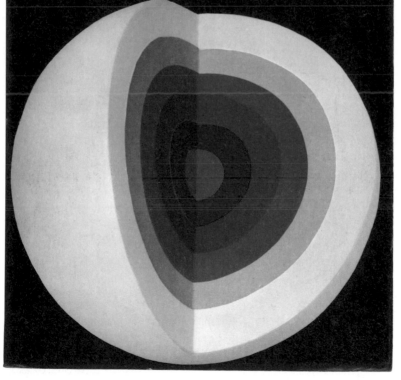

E.J.Hobsbawm/George Rudé
Captain Swing

Penguin Crime 3/6

The scarlet letters

Ellery Queen

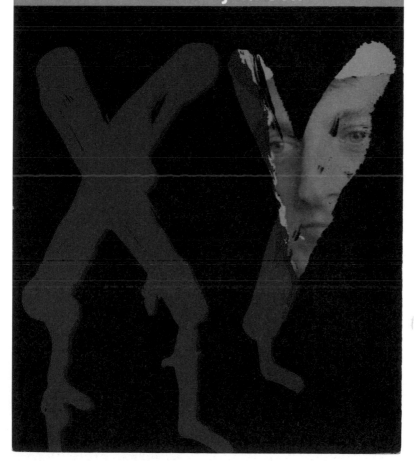

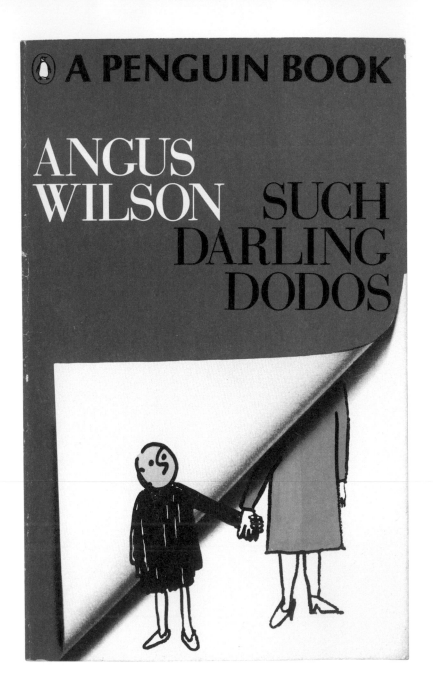

André Gide

The Immoralist

a Pelican Book   6/-

The Triple Thinkers

Edmund Wilson

Penguin Modern Classics

James Joyce

A Portrait of the Artist as a Young Man

George Steiner
Tolstoy or Dostoevsky

a Peregrine Book

BERTOLT BRECHT

PARABLES
FOR THE THEATRE

The Good Woman of Setzuan
The Caucasian Chalk Circle

4/6

Penguin Crime

3/6

Hangman's holiday

Dorothy L. Sayers

Penguin Modern Classics

Brave New World
Aldous Huxley

PENGUIN BOOKS

THE
PLAGUE

Albert Camus

COMPLETE **3/6** UNABRIDGED

Penguin Crime

3/-

Coffin,
scarcely used

Colin Watson

The Penguin English Library

WILKIE COLLINS
THE MOONSTONE

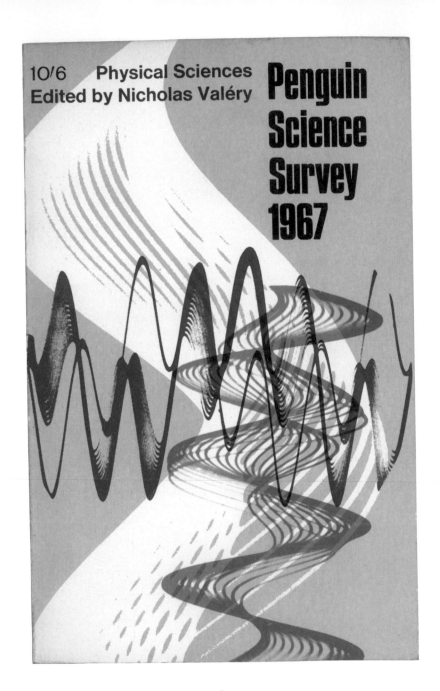

10/6 Physical Sciences
Edited by Nicholas Valéry

**Penguin
Science
Survey
1967**

a Pelican Book 3/6

What is History?

E. H. Carr

a Pelican Book   5'-

The Origins and
Growth of Biology

Edited by Arthur Rook

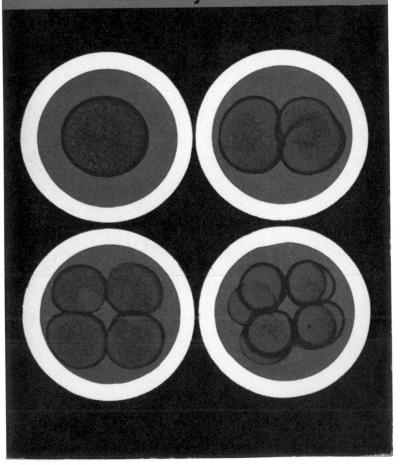

penguin science survey

B

1963

7/6

Penguin Crime 5/-

Have his carcase

Dorothy L. Sayers

a Pelican Original

The Strange Case of Pot

Michael Schofield

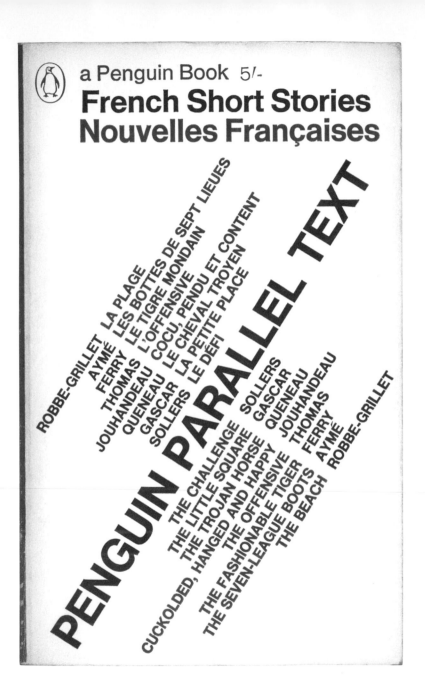

A PENGUIN SPECIAL

LOUIS LÉVY

THE TRUTH ABOUT FRANCE

Translated by
W. PICKLES

PINGÜINO

MATEO LUJÁN DE SAYAVEDRA
ANTONIO VILLEGAS

Novelistas Anteriores
a Cervantes

clásicos clásicos

LAUTARO

LA FRANCE GUERRIÈRE

Choisie par

LEWIS THORPE

RECONNAISSANCE
KAPKA KASSABOVA

A NOVEL

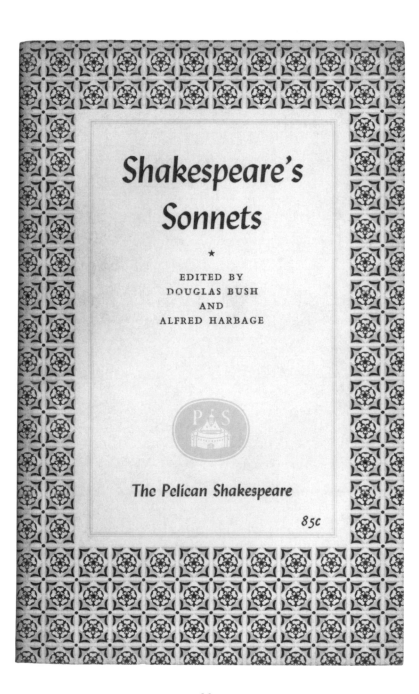

Shakespeare's
Sonnets

★

EDITED BY
DOUGLAS BUSH
AND
ALFRED HARBAGE

The Pelican Shakespeare

85c

'A brilliantly and preposterously funny book' *Guardian*

a home at the
end of the world

'One of the finest novels I have read in years'
John Banville, *Observer*

michael
cunningham

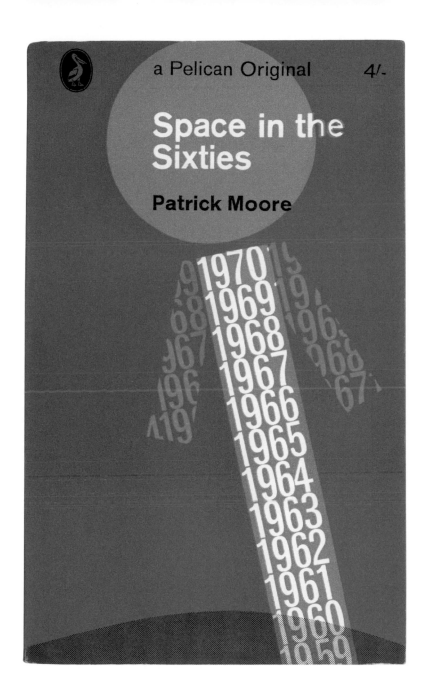

a Pelican Original   4/-

Space in the Sixties

Patrick Moore

ERLE STANLEY GARDNER

THE CASE
OF THE SILENT PARTNER

PENGUIN BOOKS 2/6

670

A PENGUIN SPECIAL

ALAN THOMPSON
AND
CLAUDE H. GOODCHILD

KEEPING
POULTRY
AND
RABBITS
ON SCRAPS

Intimate Strangers

NEW STORIES FROM QUEBEC

Edited by
Matt Cohen & Wayne Grady

PENGUIN · SHORT · FICTION

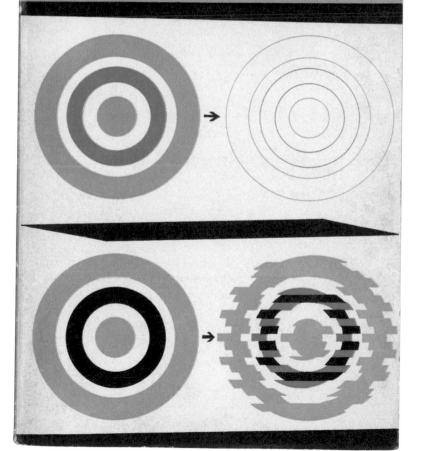

Penguin Crime

3/6

Hare sitting up

Michael Innes

A PENGUIN SPECIAL

WARTIME "GOOD HOUSEKEEPING" COOKERY BOOK

Compiled by

GOOD HOUSEKEEPING INSTITUTE

SCIENCE
NEWS 53

PENGUIN BOOKS 2/6

Ancient Sorceries and
other stories
Algernon Blackwood

Penguin Crime 3/6

Slow Burner

William Haggard

a Penguin Perry Mason 2/6

The case of the shoplifter's shoe

Erle Stanley Gardner

GOETHE

FAUST

PART ONE

A NEW TRANSLATION
BY PHILIP WAYNE

1/6

KING PENGUIN

YUKIO MISHIMA
THE SAILOR WHO FELL FROM GRACE WITH THE SEA

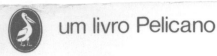

um livro Pelicano

A Psicologia da Aprendizagem

Robert Borger e A.E.M. Seaborne

Penguin Crime 3/6

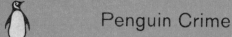

The Haunted Monastery

Robert van Gulik

JUDGE DEE in another ancient
Chinese detective story

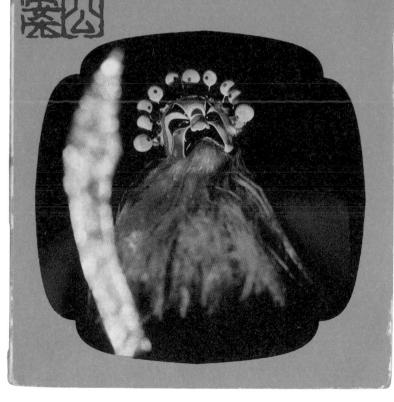

a Pelican Original 3/6

Soviet Education

Nigel Grant

THE BIRTH AND DEATH OF MEANING

SECOND EDITION

ERNEST BECKER

ALBERT CAMUS

The Outsider

The New Industrial State

Industrial State

John Kenneth Galbraith

The Heart of
the Matter

Graham Greene

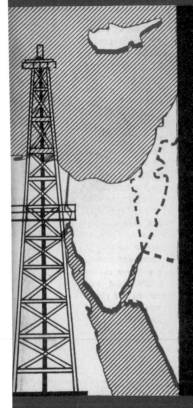

A Penguin Special

GUY WINT and
PETER CALVOCORESSI

Middle
East
Crisis

The series of events which
preceded the recent crisis in
the Middle East, and proposals
for future Western policy

2/-

a Pelican Book

Superman and Common Men
Freedom, Anarchy and
the Revolution
Benjamin R. Barber

Saint-Exupéry

Flight to Arras

PENGUIN MODERN CLASSICS

2'6

LOS
ANGELES

THE ARCHITECTURE OF FOUR ECOLOGIES

REYNER BANHAM

GEORGE ORWELL

Nineteen Eighty-Four

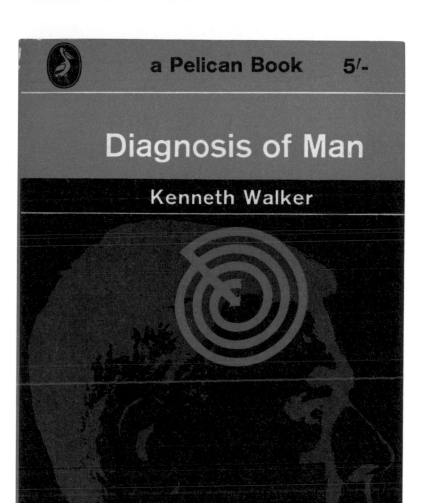

a Pelican Book 5/-

Diagnosis of Man

Kenneth Walker

Penguin Crime 3'6

The adventures of Ellery Queen

Ellery Queen

HOYLE

Hubert Phillips

* BRIDGE * WHIST * PONTOON *
PARTY GAMES
CRIBBAGE * DRAUGHTS * CANASTA * RUMMY
HOGGENHEIMER * PIQUET *
* POKER * BEZIQUE * PATIENCE *

A Book of Indoor Games

5/-

PENGUIN
BOOKS

FICTION

GREY
AREA

—

WILL SELF

FICTION

a Pelican Book   3/6

a pictorial history of **Nazi Germany**

Erwin Leiser

A
PENGUIN SPECIAL

FOOD

THE
DECIDING
FACTOR

A Guide to Rationing
and Food Values

By Frank Wokes

Index

Where practicable, cover credits are reproduced exactly as found on the back of the
book, hence the variation in style and the occasional uncredited cover design

702

90. *Man and Automation*, 1957. Cover illustration by Erwin Fabian

91. *Put Out the Light*, 1946

92. *The Cruel Sea*, 1980. Cover illustration by Phil Wright

93. *The Quiet American*, 1962. Cover drawing by Paul Hogarth

94. *Hackenfeller's Ape*, 1968. Cover design by Michael Levey

95. *The Great Gatsby*, 1974. Cover design by John Gorham

96. *The Dog it was that Died*, 1966. Cover design by C/F/F/G

97. *Jubb*, 1966. Cover photographs by Richard Heimann

98. *The Farewell Party*, 1977

99. *Penguin Modern Poets 26*, 1975. Cover photograph by Tony Evans

100. *The Battle is the Pay-Off*, 1943. All illustrations courtesy the newspaper *PM*

101. *What I'm Going to Do, I Think*, 1972. Cover design by Tony Meeuwissen

102. *Take a Girl Like You*, 1975. Cover drawing by Quentin Blake

103. *De Valera*, 1939. The portrait on the cover is by Howard Coster

104. *A Tree of Night*, 1967. Cover photograph by Graphic Display Unit. Engraving reproduced by kind permission of Mary Evans Picture Library

105. *Maigret Sets a Trap*, 1968. Cover by John Hughes

106. *Bestseller*, 1975. Cover design by John Gorham

107. *Kiss Kiss*, 1966. Cover design by Aldridge/Rolfe

108. *Harris in Wonderland*, 1976. Cover design by Mary Barnes

109. *Jamaica Inn*, 1972. Cover illustration by Charles Raymond

110. *Old Junk*, 1944

111. *I Should Have Stayed Home*, 1966. Cover photograph by Harri Peccinotti

112. *Fantasy-Overture Romeo and Juliet*, 1951. Cover designed by Kissane Keane

113. *The Heckler*, 1966. Cover design by Tony Palladino

114. *The Long March*, 1964. Cover design by Milton Glaser

115. *Herzog*, 1965. Cover design by Tony Palladino

116. *Threepenny Novel*, 1976. The cover, designed by Germano Facetti, shows a detail from 'The Matchseller' by Otto Dix, in the State Gallery, Stuttgart

117. *Medicine Today*, 1961. Cover design by John Griffiths

118. *The Origins of the Second World War*, 1964. Cover design by Tom Eckersley. Photo: Associated Press

119. *Watership Down*, 1978. The cover design incorporates a still from the film *Watership Down*. Written for the screen, produced and directed by Martin Rosen. Produced by Nepenthe Productions Limited

120. *A Burnt-Out Case*, 1966. Cover photograph by Ronald Traeger

121. *A Night of Errors*, 1966. Cover design by Lou Klein

122. *The Rise of the Meritocracy, 1870–2033*, 1961. Cover by Hans Unger

123. *The Prevalence of Witches*, 1957. Cover illustration by Abram Games

124. *The Drunken Forest*, 1971

125. *Nineteen Eighty-Four*, 1983. Cover design by Carroll & Dempsey Limited

126. *The Menstrual Cycle*, 1969. Cover design by Mike Pope

127. *A Severed Head*, 1963. Cover design by Charles Raymond

128. *Take These Men*, 1956

129. *Group Portrait with Lady*, 1976. Cover Illustration by Candy Amsden

130. *The Penguin Feiffer*, 1964. Design by Brian Dunn

131. *A Summer Birdcage*, 1979. Cover photograph by Chris Yates

132. *New Biology 22*, 1957

133. *I, Claudius*, 1985. Cover illustration by Brida Pike

134. *Mother Wore Tights*, 1947. Illustrated by Howard Williamson

135. *The Sound and the Fury*, 1965. Cover drawing by André François

136. *A Dictionary of Electronics*, 1962. Cover design by Alan Fletcher

137. *My Fair Lady*, 1975. Cover photograph by Cecil Beaton

138. *A Scandalous Woman*, 1976. Cover photograph by Barry Lategan

139. *Murder Makes the Wheels Go Round*, 1970. Cover design by Head Office

140. *My Turn to Make the Tea*, 1965. Cover design by John Ward

141. *God in Action*, 1961. Cover design by Bernard Baker

142. *Hopjoy Was Here*, 1966. Cover design by Brian Haynes

143. *Room at the Top*, 1959

144. *Days of Wine and Rage*, 1980. Cover illustration by Neil Curtis

145. *The Case of the Rolling Bones*, 1966. Cover painting by Giannetto Coppola

146. *Ada*, 1980. The cover, designed by Carroll & Dempsey, shows a detail from 'Untitled No. 1, 1962' by Richard Lindner.

Reproduced by kind permission of Mr & Mrs Morton G. Neumann. Photograph © Harry N. Abrams Inc. New York

147. *The Wild Palms*, 1975. The cover shows a detail from 'The Waiting Room' by George Tooker, in the National Collection of Fine Arts, Washington

148. *Spinster*, 1961

149. *The D.A. Holds a Candle*, 1957. Cover illustration by Edwin Tatum

150. *The Snows of Kilimanjaro*, 1963. Cover design by Paul Hogarth

151. *Voltaire in Love*, 1960. Cover illustration by Cecil Beaton

152. *Inside Mr Enderby*, 1979. Cover design by Peter Bentley

153. *Sunshine Sketches of a Little Town*, 1944

154. *Sweet Dreams*, 1976. Cover illustration by Philip Castle

155. *Time Out of Joint*, 1976. Cover illustration by Peter Tybus

156. *The Unpleasant Profession of Jonathan Hoag*, 1966. Cover illustration by Alan Aldridge

157. *The American Way of Death*, 1963

158. *Flower-Growing for Shows*, 1959. Cover design by David Gentleman

159. *Art and its Objects*, 1970. Cover design by John Golding

160. *Two Adolescents*, 1969. Cover illustration by Ken Sequin

161. *A Special Case?*, 1972. Cover design: Omnific/ Derek Birdsall

162. *America the Vincible*, 1960

163. *Helter Skelter*, 1977. Cover photograph by Robert Hendrickson (John Hillelson Agency)

164. *Fidel Castro Speaks*, 1972. Cover design Mike Pope

165. *Gerard Manley Hopkins*, 1964

166. *The Inferno*, 1979. Cover illustration by Adrian Chesterman

167. *The Organization Man*, 1961. Cover design by Erwin Fabian

168. *The Penguin Cookery Book*, 1965. Cover photograph by Ian Yeomans

169. *The Culture of the Abdomen*, 1957. Cover design by Margaret Belsky

170. *As You Like It*, 1959

171. *Browning*, 1964. Cover design by Stephen Russ

172. *The Penguin Dictionary of Archaeology*, 1988. Cover design by Carroll & Dempsey Limited incorporates an early Athenian urn c. 540 B.C.

173. *The Penguin Car Handbook*, 1960. Cover design by Erwin Fabian

174. *China*, 1960. Cover photograph copyright by Henri Cartier-Bresson

175. *Lolita*, 1980. Cover photograph from the MGM release 'Lolita' © 1962

176. *The Condition of English Schooling*, 1979. Cover design: Jones Thompson, Design Associates

177. *The Penguin Handbook of First Aid*, 1961. Cover design by Hans Unger

178. *Bird Recognition*, 1947

179. *More Comic & Curious Verse*, 1964. Cover design by Stephen Russ

180. *The Fourth Stage of Gainsborough Brown*, 1978. Cover design by Paul Bacon

181. *British Poetry since 1945*, 1970. The cover shows a detail from an untitled painting by Rolf Brandt

182. *The Penguin Dictionary of Computers*, 1985. Cover photographs: Science Photo Library

183. *Hurry on Down*, 1963. Cover by Gillian Lewis

184. *Escape Attempts*, 1978. Cover illustration by Ralph Steadman

185. *A History of the U.S.S.R.*, 1950

186. *The First Year of Teaching*, 1976. Cover design: Martin Causer

187. *Soft Fruit Growing*, 1945

188. *A Salute to the Great McCarthy*, 1974. Cover design: Tucker & James

189. *The Dog-Exercising Machine*, 1971. Cover illustration by Michael Burns de Bono

190. *Endless Pressure*, 1979. Cover photo: Steve Herr

191. *The Penguin Book of Canadian Verse*, 1967. Cover design by Nicoletta Baroni

192. *The Penguin Dictionary of Building*, 1978. Cover design: Omnific

193. *An Outline of European Architecture*, 1945

194. *Frame Analysis*, 1975

195. *Explorations*, 1964. Cover design by Graham Bishop

196. *Atlas of World Population History*, 1978. Cover illustration: Michael Foreman

197. *Mallarmé*, 1965

198. *A Dictionary of Science*, 1964. Cover design by Fletcher/Forbes/Gill

199. *Gardening the Modern Way*, 1962. The cover illustration is of Clare College garden in Cambridge, and is reproduced by kind permission of the Master and Fellows of the College

257. *Money & Banking*, 1973. Cover design: Omnific/ Derek Birdsall

258. *The Poetry of Experience*, 1974. Cover design by John McConnell

259. *Noise*, 1970. Cover design by Mel Calman and Philip Thompson

260. *The Penguin Book of Health and Beauty Recipes*, 1958

261. *The Australian Ugliness*, 1963. The cover illustration is by the author

262. *Bhowani Junction*, 1971. Cover design by Steve Dwoskin

263. *The Kaiser and His Times*, 1975. The cover photograph shows Kaiser Wilhelm II posing for an equestrian portrait (Archiv Gerstenberg, Frankfurt-am-Main)

264. *William Carlos Williams*, 1976. Cover design by Wendy Taylor, based on a photo by John D. Schiff

265. *Only Yesterday*, 1938

266. *War and Peace: 1*, 1977. The cover shows Alan Dobie as Andrei in the television version of *War and Peace* co-produced by the British Broadcasting Corporation and Time-Life Films. Photograph by Lief Ericksenn

267. *Personality*, 1972. Cover design: Omnific/George Mayhew

268. *The Other America*, 1968. Cover design by Roy Kuhlman

269. *Other Men's Flowers*, 1960

270. *Preserves for All Occasions*, 1953

271. *Sailing*, 1958

272. *Usage and Abusage*, 1963. Cover design by Derek Birdsall

273. *Time for School*, 1973

274. *Health of the Future*, 1942

275. *Understanding and Helping the Schizophrenic*, 1981. Cover design by Andrew Wadsworth. Photographs by David Fairman

276. *Revolt into Style*, 1972. The cover shows the painting 'The Beatles 1962' by Peter Blake from the collection of Colin St John Wilson

277. *The Penguin Dictionary of Physics*, 1980. Cover design: Martin Causer

278. *The Spare-Time Book*, 1961. Cover design by David Gentleman

279. *The Personality of Animals*, 1943

280. *In Search of England*, 1960. Cover illustration by Sylvia Stokeld

281. *The Chess Mind*, 1960. Cover design by George Him

282. *A Critical Dictionary of Psychoanalysis*, 1979. Cover design: Omnific. Drawing: André François

283. *Pulsar: 1*, 1978. Cover illustration by Adrian Chesterman

284. *Pygmalion*, 1957

285. *The Case of the Howling Dog*, 1963. Cover design by Romek Marber

286. *Schultz*, 1980. Cover illustrations by George Sharpe

287. *The Mersey Sound*, 1985. Cover design: Trickett and Webb Limited. Cover photograph by Dmitri Kasterine

288. *Sociolinguistics*, 1986. Cover design by Antonio Verdi

289. *The Sun Chemist*, 1978. Cover photographs by Robert Golden

290. *Troilus and Cressida*, 1988. cover illustration by Paul Hogarth

291. *Red Harvest*, 1963. Cover design by Romek Marber

292. *Ski Holidays in the Alps*, 1961

293. *British Economic Policy Since the War*, 1958. Cover illustration by Erwin Fabian

294. *A Book of English Poetry*, 1950

295. *The Well*, 1987. Cover design by Neil Stuart/Cover illustration by Pamela Noftsinger

296. *Hot Sand*, 1997. Cover photograph © Austral International

297. *A Dictionary of Electronics*, 1971. The Cover shows an integrated circuit mask much enlarged (Motorola Semiconductor Products Inc)

298. *Europe in Chains*, 1940

299. *Language and Social Context*, 1979. Cover design: Omnific/Martin Causer

300. *Madame Prunier's Fish Cook Book*, 1963. Cover design by Bruce Robertson. Photograph by Ian Yeomans

301. *Driving Made Easy*, 1980. Cover design by Jones Thompson

302. *Maternal Deprivation Reassessed*, 1979. Cover design: Omnific

303. *Caesars of the Wilderness*, 1988. Jacket design: V. John Lee. Illustration: A. Sherriff Scott

304. *Improve Your Soccer*, 1966. Cover design by Bruce Robertson. Photograph by Ken Coton

305. *The French Canadians Today*, 1942

306. *Mao Tse-Tung Unrehearsed*, 1974. The cover, designed by David King, shows a detail from a poster issued by the Chinese People's Republic.

307. *A Dictionary of Science*, 1954

308. *Bridge*, 1961. Cover design by George Him

309. *A Diary of World Affairs*, 1941
310. *No Signposts in the Sea*, 1965. Cover painting by Giannetto Coppola
311. *The Maltese Falcon*, 1963. Cover design by Romek Marber
312. *The Film Director as Superstar*, 1974. Cover design by Peter Fluck
313. *No More Meadows*, 1970. Cover illustration by Michael Johnson
314. *This Slimming Business*, 1962. Cover design by Patrick Tilley
315. *Maigret and the Burglar's Wife*, 1961. Cover design by Romek Marber
316. *Damned Whores and God's Police*, 1975. The cover, designed by Pam Brewster, shows an original painting by Ruth Gregory
317. *The Raining Tree War*, 1977. Cover illustration by Peter Bentley
318. *Searchlight on Spain*, 1938
319. *Highland Dress*, 1948
320. *A Wine Primer*, 1973. Cover photograph by John Bulmer
321. *Antibodies and Immunity*, 1971. Cover design by Mel Calman and Philip Thompson
322. *Ethics*, 1978. The cover shows a relief of Pallas Athene in the National Museum in Athens
323. *The Supernatural Omnibus*, 1976. Cover illustration by Justin Todd
324. *The Singing Sands*, 1977. Cover photograph by Paul Wakefield
325. *Unemployment*, 1979. Cover design by Jones Thompson
326. *Coming Up for Air*, 1962. Cover design by Alan Fletcher

327. *Cousin Bette*, 1973. The cover shows a detail from 'La Lecture' by Fantin-Latour in the Musée de Lyon (Snark International)
328. *Cold War and Counter-Revolution*, 1976. Cover design by Robert Geissmann. Cover painting by Christopher Davis
329. *The Agricola and the Germania*, 1985. The cover shows a detail from a relief on a gravestone, in the National Museum, Rome
330. *Cambao – The Yoke*, 1972. The cover, designed by Germano Facetti, shows a detail from 'Slave' by José Clemente Orozco in the Huntingdon Hartford Gallery of Modern Art, New York (Bisonte)
331. *P O: Beyond Yes & No*, 1975. Cover design by David Pelham
332. *The Image in Form*, 1972. The cover shows a colonnade in the courtyard of the ducal palace of Urbino (photo Felicitas Vogler)
333. *The Imitation of Christ*, 1965. Cover based on a detail from the title-page woodcut of Dürer's Apocalypse (photos British Museum)
334. *Billy Liar*, 1970. Cover illustration by Paul Psorakis
335. *Congo Disaster*, 1961. Cover design by Juliet Renny
336. *Married Life in an African Tribe*, 1971. Cover photograph by USPG
337. *Class in a Capitalist Society*, 1980. Cover design by Jones Thompson
338. *Leave it to Cook*, 1975. Cover photograph by Bob Brookes
339. *The Best of Beachcomber*, 1966. Cover illustrations by Edda Köchl
340. *The Intelligent Woman's*

Guide to Atomic Radiation, 1964. Cover design by Bruce Robertson
341. *Russian Cookery*, 1968. Cover photograph taken at the Restaurant National, Moscow (Novosti)
342. *Design as Art*, 1971. Cover design by Bruno Munari
343. *Your Child's Room*, 1965. Cover photograph by Knöppel (Camera Press)
344. *Mothers and Working Mothers*, 1979. Cover illustration Michelle Haynes, aged 8
345. *Maldoror*, 1978. The cover shows a detail from 'The Deluge' by Joshua Shaw, in the Metropolitan Museum of Art, New York
346. *Wuthering Heights*, 1964. Cover drawing by Paul Hogarth
347. *The Great Gatsby*, 1982. The cover shows a detail from 'Montparno's Blues' by Kees Van Dongen, in a private collection (Snark International)
348. *Cicero: Selected Works*, 1969. The cover shows a bust of Cicero, of the first century B.C., in the Wellington Museum (photo Rodney Todd-White)
349. *Jake's Thing*, 1980. Cover design by Neil Stuart. Cover illustration by Brian Forbes
350. *The Pyramids of Egypt*, 1964. The cover design by Bruce Robertson incorporates a photograph of a wooden model in the British Museum, about 1400 B.C.
351. *Dignity and Purity*, 1966. Cover photographs by Dennis Jackson
352. *Work Suspended*, 1981. Cover design by Peter Bentley
353. *Self-Love*, 1972. Cover design by Jeannette Cissman

354. *Night Flight*, 1945

355. *The Grass is Singing*, 1969. Cover design by Goodwin/Sorrell

356. *The Biocrats*, 1972. The cover shows a seven-week living human foetus (photo Landrum B. Shettles, M.D., Ph.D., D.Sc., F.A.C.S., F.A.C.O.G., F.R.S.H.)

357. *The Empty Space*, 1972. The cover, designed by Germano Facetti, shows a scene from the RSC production of *A Midsummer Night's Dream*, directed by Peter Brook (Photo Max Waldmann)

358. *Improve Your Rugby*, 1967. Cover design by Bruce Robertson

359. *The Penguin Book of Ballads*, 1975. Cover photograph by Trevor Wood

360. *Live Now, Pay Later*, 1963. Cover design by Martin Bassett

361. *The Mabinogion*, 1976. The cover shows a detail from 'The Four Queens' by David Jones, in the Tate Gallery, London (photo John Webb, London), © the Trustees of W. D. Jones, 1976

362. *The Night of Kadar*, 1979. Cover illustration by Adrian Chesterman

363. *The Parent's Schoolbook*, 1976. Cover design by John Gorham

364. *Italian Fascism*, 1975. Cover design by David Pelham (photos Keystone Press Agency, London)

365. *Rich Against Poor*, 1975. Cover design by Jones Thompson

366. *Further Rivals of Sherlock Holmes*, 1976. Cover design by John Gorham

367. *Alcestis and Other Plays*, 1964. The cover shows a marble relief from the Temple of Jupiter at Olympia (Snark Archives)

368. *1905*, 1973. The cover shows a Russian poster of 1906, 'The spirit of the murdered workers, unappeased by the promise of a new constitution, cries out for revenge and revolution', by permission of the Society for Cultural Relations with the U.S.S.R. (photo Rodney Todd-White)

369. *The Penguin Book of English Romantic Verse*, 1983. The cover shows a detail of 'Horse Frightened by Lion' by George Stubbs, in the Walker Art Gallery, Liverpool

370. *False Colours*, 1971. Cover design by James Torney

371. *God is Not Yet Dead*, 1973. Cover design by Enzo Ragazzini

372. *A Random State*, 1973. Cover painting by Bengt Nystrom

373. *Asylums*, 1982. Cover design by Briggs and McLaren

374. *Escape to Switzerland*, 1945

375. *Mountaineering*, 1968. Cover design by Bruce Robertson

376. *Glass Through the Ages*, 1959

377. *The Grey Flannel Shroud*, 1963. Cover design by Martin Bassett

378. *The Contenders*, 1969. Cover photograph by Dennis Rolfe

379. *Roses*, 1970

380. *The Blood of Others*, 1966. Cover illustration by Giannetto Coppola

381. *The Runner's Handbook*, 1983. Cover design by Neil Stuart/Cover photograph courtesy of Photo Researchers, Inc.

382. *Evolution and Revolution*, 1974

383. *Quintessence*, 1999. Photograph TRANZ/Photonica. Cover design Dexter Fry

384. *Hardy Bulbs 2*, 1964. Cover photograph of mixed narcissi by J. E. Downward

385. *Picasso*, 1971. The cover, designed by Germano Facetti, shows a portrait photo of Pablo Picasso by Marc Riboud (Magnum)

386. *Portrait of Jennie*, 1947

387. *God's Little Acre*, 1947

388. *Britain in the Sixties: Housing*, 1962. Cover photograph by Jane Gate

389. *Chéri* and *The Last of Chéri*, 1974. Cover design by Walter Brooks

390. *Geology and Scenery in Ireland*, 1974. Cover photograph by Alan Spain, showing the cliffs of Moher, County Clare

391. *Medieval Latin Lyrics*, 1968. The cover shows a detail from an eleventh-century plainsong manuscript in the Bibliothèque Nationale, Paris (Snark International)

392. *Brazil: The People and the Power*, 1972. Cover photograph by Enzo Ragazzini

393. *Great Son*, 1947

394. *The Ambassadress*, 1965. Cover painting by Giannetto Coppola

395. *Existentialism*, 1976

396. *The Great Terror*, 1971. The cover shows a detail from a satirical drawing by Th. Th. Heine, published 1927 in *Simplizissimus* (Bisonte)

397. *Further Fables for Our Time*, 1962

398. *Len Deighton's London Dossier*, 1967

399. *The Loss of El Dorado*,

Wright. Photograph by Karl Ferris

455. *The New Architecture of Europe*, 1962. The photographs on the front cover show the Phönix-Rheinrohr Building in Düsseldorf, reproduced by permission of Arno Wrubel, and the Notre-Dame du Haut at Ronchamp

456. *The Night of Wenceslas*, 1962. Cover drawing by Romek Marber

457. *Gascoyne*, 1969. Cover design by Michael Trevithick

458. *Statistics Without Tears*, 1991

459. *Penguin Modern Poets 24*, 1974. Cover photograph by Jean-Louis Bloch-Lainé

460. *The Connoisseur's Crossword Book*, 1967. Cover design by J. Larkin

461. *Man and the Vertebrates: 1*, 1974. Cover painting by Michael Johnson

462. *For the Liberation of Brazil*, 1971

463. *La Tierra del Bien-Te-Veo*, 1948

464. *Skin and Hair Care*, 1978. Cover illustration by Philip Castle, was originated by Chetwynd Advertising for Pantene professional hairstyling products

465. *Survive the Savage Sea*, 1974. Cover photograph by Humphrey Sutton

466. *The Concept of Mind*, 1966. Cover design by Romek Marber

467. *Arrival and Departure*, 1969. Cover design by David Pelham

468. *The Lotus and the Wind*, 1958. Cover illustration by Denis Piper

469. *The Jazz Scene*, 1961. Cover by Alan Fletcher

470. *The Joyful Community*, 1973. Cover design by Roy La Grone

471. *Evolution in Action*, 1963. Cover design by Bruce Robertson

472. *The Diary of a Nobody*, 1945

473. *Penguin Modern Poets 22*, 1973. Cover design by Alan Spain

474. *Metamorphosis*, 1965. Cover drawing by Yosl Bergner

475. *Generals and Generalship*, 1941

476. *The Hunter and the Whale*, 1977. Cover design by David King

477. *Adolf Hitler – My Part in His Downfall*, 1982. *Adolf Hitler – My Part in His Downfall* is a Norman Cohen film, produced by Gregory Smith and Norman Cohen and directed by Norman Cohen. The film stars Jim Dale, Arthur Lowe and Bill Maynard, with Spike Milligan as Guest Star. A United Artists release

478. *Instead of Education*, 1977. Cover design by Christine Johnson

479. *Ten Days that Shook the World*, 1966

480. *The Penguin Book of Elizabethan Verse*, 1971. Cover design by Stephen Russ

481. *Ripening Seed*, 1961. Cover illustration by Vernon J. Murrell

482. *The Deceivers*, 1957. Cover illustration by David Caplan

483. *Nineteen Eighty-Four*, 1960

484. *H. G. Wells: Selected Short Stories*, 1958

485. *Literacy and Development in the West*, 1969. Cover design by Bruce Robertson

486. *The Reefs of Space*, 1969. Cover design by Franco Gignani

487. *Goodbye to All That*, 1965. Cover drawing by Paul Hogarth

488. *Summer Cooking*, 1965. Cover photograph by Anthony Denney

489. *The Case of Torches*, 1963. Cover design by George Daulby

490. *The Grass Harp/In Cold Blood/Breakfast at Tiffany's*, 1966

491. *Stranger in the House*, 1967. The cover shows James Mason, Geraldine Chaplin and Bobby Darin, the stars of the de Grunwald production 'Stranger in the House'. Produced by Dimitri de Grunwald and directed by Pierre Rouve in Eastman Colour

492. *Mister Johnson*, 1968. Cover drawing by Julian Allen

493. *Anatomy of a Murder*, 1960

494. *Poverty*, 1972. Cover design: Omnific/Derek Birdsall

495. *The Great Gatsby*, [>1998]

496. *Heaven & Hell*, 1938

497. *Penguin Survey of Business and Industry*, 1965

498. *Yet More Comic & Curious Verse*, 1964. Cover design by Stephen Russ

499. *The Mackerel Plaza*, 1963. Cover design by Derek Birdsall

500. *A Room of One's Own*, 1945

501. *W. H. Auden*, 1958

502. *Understanding Weather*, 1961. Cover design by Derek Birdsall

503. *In Cold Blood*, 1970. Cover design by David Pelham

504. *The Little Fishes*, 1966. Cover design by Michael Peters

505. *Intonation*, 1972. Cover

design: Omnific/Michael Foreman

506. *Listening and Attention*, 1969. Cover design by Snark International

507. *The Railway Accident and Other Stories*, 1972. The cover, designed by Germano Facetti, shows 'Time Transfixed' by René Magritte, reproduced by courtesy of the Art Institute of Chicago

508. *Do You Sincerely Want to be Rich?*, 1972. Cover design by John McConnell

509. *The Cloud of Unknowing*, 1961

510. *The Penguin Book of English Verse*, 1966. Cover design by Stephen Russ

511. *Life in a Secondary Modern School*, 1970. Cover design by Patrick McCreeth

512. *Lost in the Funhouse*, 1972. Cover by Eduardo Paolozzi

513. *The Wapshot Chronicle*, 1963. Cover design by Derek Birdsall

514. *The Outsider*, [>1998]. Cover design: Arber @ Public Art Creative Consultants Limited

515. *The Penguin Problems Book*, 1940

516. *Yevtushenko: Selected Poems*, 1963. Cover design by Barrett

517. *The Book of Laughter and Forgetting*, 1985. Cover illustration by Andrzej Klimowski

518. *Penguin Science Survey B: 1966*, 1966. Cover design by Henrion

519. *The Uses of Literacy*, 1963. Cover design by Romek Marber

520. *Poem into Poem*, 1970. Cover design by Germano Facetti

521. *Transport*, 1968. Cover design by B. E. Rockett

522. *The Penguin Book of Japanese Verse*, 1964. Cover pattern by Stephen Russ

523. *The Literary Critics* 1962. Cover design by Derek Birdsall

524. *The Penguin Dictionary of Saints*, 1965. Cover shows a detail from an illuminated Book of Hours in the National Library, Florence (Snark International)

525. *Le Zéro et L'Infini*, 1946

526. *Billy Liar*, 19/3. Cover design by Tony Meeuwissen

527. *All's Well That End's Well*, 1970. Cover design by David Gentleman

528. *The Senses*, 1966. Cover design by Bruce Robertson

529. *Landscape with Dead Dons*, 1963. Cover design by Sheila Perry

530. *A Book of English Poetry*, 1938

531. *Another India*, 1990. Cover design by Amiya Bhattacharya

532. *Goodbye to All That*, [>1998]. Cover design: Intro

533. *To Kill a Mockingbird*, 1965. Cover design by Derek Birdsall

534. *The Koran*, 1956

535. *A Guide to English Schools*, 1964. Cover design by Alan Aldridge

536. *Brief Candles*, 1965. Cover design by Alan Spain, distortion by Nelson Christmas

537. *The Common Pursuit*, 1966

538. *Reading, How to*, 1974. Cover design: Omnific/ Derek Birdsall

539. *Monopolies and Restrictive Practices*, 1968. Cover design by Martin Bassett

540. *The Penguin John Lennon*, 1973. Cover photograph by David Nutter

541. *William Morris: Selected Writings and Designs*, 1962. Cover illustration based on a William Morris honeysuckle chintz

542. *Penguin Modern Poets 20*, 1972. Cover design by Alan Spain

543. *The Rains Came*, 1959. Cover Illustration by Brian Keogh

544. *Hitler*, 1971. Cover design by Frederick Price

545. *The Pañćatantra*, 1993. Cover illustration by Shalinee Ghosh. Cover design by Bena Sareen

546. *A Puzzle for Pilgrims*, 1986. Cover photograph by Ian Hooten

547. *The Innocence of Father Brown*, 1962. Cover design by Romek Marber

548. *The Magic Christian*, 1969. Cover shows Peter Sellers and Ringo Starr, stars of 'The Magic Christian', produced by Denis O'Dell and directed by Joseph McGrath. Released by Commonwealth United Entertainment Inc. Cover design by Bob Gill

549. *The Glass Village*, 1963. Cover design by Romek Marber

550. *Socialization*, 1976. Cover design: Omnific/ Dennis Bailey

551. *Only One Earth*, 1972. Cover design by Brian Mayers (photograph by NASA)

552. *Penguin Modern Poets 17*, 1970. Cover photograph by Alan Spain

553. *A High-Pitched Buzz*, 1962. Cover design by Derek Birdsall. Drawing by Quentin Blake

554. *Industrial Man*, 1969. Cover design by Peter Stone

555. *My Oedipus Complex*, 1978. Cover design by Omnific

556. *Penguin Modern Playwrights: 2*, 1966. Cover design by Germano Facetti
557. *The Management of Government*, 1972. Cover design by Peter Smith
558. *Robert Herrick*, 1961
559. *Browning*, 1981. The cover shows a detail of 'The Coliseum by Moonlight' by Frederick Lee Bridell, in the City of Southampton Art Gallery (photo Cumberland Studio)
560. *The Penguin Book of English Verse*, 1982. The cover shows a detail from a portrait of Elizabeth Fitzgerald, Countess of Lincoln, by Steven van der Meulen, in a private collection (photo Rodney Todd-White, London)
561. *Samuel Taylor Coleridge*, 1957
562. *An Awkward Life*, 1985. Cover design by Neil Stuart/ Cover photograph by Arthur Tress
563. *Spin and Other Turns*, 1994. Cover illustration by Pavan Buragohain. Cover design by Ray & Keshavan Design Associates
564. *The Joys of Yiddish*, 1988. Cover design by David Pelham
565. *Murder is Easy*, 1957. Cover illustration by Stanley Godsell
566. *The Sandcastle*, 1963. Cover drawing by Terence Greer
567. *Language, Truth and Logic*, 1971. Cover design by John Smith
568. *Tiger! Tiger!*, 1974. Cover illustration by David Pelham
569. *On the Road*, 1991. The cover shows Neal Cassady and Jack Kerouac reproduced by courtesy of Carolyn Cassady
570. *The New Poetry*, 1980.

The cover shows Jackson Pollock's 'Convergence' (Albright-Knox Art Gallery, Buffalo, New York)
571. *Ethnomethodology*, 1975. Cover design: Omnific/Anthony Froshaug
572. *New Biology 16*, 1954
573. *Enemies of Promise*, 1961. The cover photograph is of Cyril Connolly
574. *Africa in Social Change*, 1972
575. *The Contemporary Cinema*, 1963. The cover design, by Tasha Kallin, incorporates a National Film Archive photograph of the making of the Unitalia film, *L'Avventura*
576. *Culture Against Man*, 1972. Cover design: Omnific/Philip Thompson
577. *Junky*, [>1998]. Design: C. Ashworth + A. Sissons. Photography: J. Holden
578. *Archaeology from the Earth*, 1961. Cover design by Bruce Robertson
579. *The Geography of African Affairs*, 1965. Cover design by George Daulby
580. *Dubliners*, 1967. The cover shows a detail of 'The Illuminated Town', by Jack B. Yeats (Victor Waddington, London: photo Rodney Todd-White)
581. *Management and the Social Sciences*, 1971. Cover design by Peter Stone
582. *Lorca*, 1960
583. *Little Herr Friedemann and Other Stories*, 1976. The cover, designed by Germano Facetti, shows a detail from a portrait of Max Hermann Neisse by George Grosz, in the Städtische Kunsthalle, Mannheim (Bisonte)
584. *Mind the Stop*, 1976. Cover design by Alan Fletcher

585. *Robert Graves*, 1968. Cover design by Stephen Russ
586. *A Last Resort?*, 1972. Cover design: Omnific
587. *Vatican Finances*, 1973. Cover design by Diagram
588. *A Charmed Life*, 1964. Cover drawing by Milton Glaser
589. *Hypnosis*, 1961. Cover design by Larry Carter
590. *Economic Justice*, 1973. Cover design: Omnific/ Anthony Froshaug
591. *The Victorian Underworld*, 1972. The cover, designed by Germano Facetti, shows a detail from a Gustave Doré engraving
592. *Dead Cert*, 1973. A Woodfall production, *Dead Cert* is directed by Tony Richardson and produced by Neil Hartley for United Artists' release
593. *Hermit of Peking*, 1979. Cover illustration by Peter Brookes
594. *Facts from Figures*, 1962. Cover design by Larry Carter
595. *Interpersonal Perception*, 1973. Cover design: Omnific/Philip Thompson
596. *Exile and the Kingdom*, 1977. Cover photograph by Henri Cartier-Bresson (The John Hillelson agency)
597. *Resistance in Europe: 1939–45*, 1976. Cover design by Sandy Field
598. *Ravan & Eddie*, 1996. Cover concept and design by Kiran Nagarkar. Cover illustration by Sondeep Poyerkar
599. *The World of Odysseus*, 1962. Cover design by Alan Spain based on a Greek vase in the British Museum
600. *The Penguin English Dictionary*, 1965. Cover design by Keith Whitehead
601. *The Case of the Careless*

Kitten, 1963. Cover design by Romek Marber

602. *Gargantua & Pantagruel*, 1965. The cover is based on an engraving by Gustave Doré

603. *The Catcher in the Rye*, 1970

604. *Man, Microbe and Malady*, 1943

605. *The Penguin Book of Canadian Verse*, 1958

606. *Britain in The Sixties: the Other England*, 1964. Cover photograph by Roger Mayne

607. *This Slimming Business*, 1977. Cover design by Steve Campbell

608. *Camping*, 1960. Cover design by Sheila M. Smith

609. *L'Assommoir*, 1985. The cover shows a detail from 'L'Absinthe', 1877, by Edgar Degas, in the Louvre (Snark International)

610. *Elephant Bill*, 1956

611. *Death at the President's Lodging*, 1966. Cover photograph by Paul Gori

612. *The Case of the Golddigger's Purse*, 1963. Cover design by Romek Marber

613. *A Dictionary of Computers*, 1970. Cover design by Germano Facetti incorporating a model by Mike Pope

614. *Zuleika Dobson*, 1981. The cover shows (reversed) one of a series of paintings of Zuleika Dobson by Sir Osbert Lancaster, © Randolph Hotel, Oxford, Trust Houses Forte Hotels Ltd

615. *The Official Sex Manual*, 1969. Cover design by Ivan Holmes

616. *Language in the Modern World*, 1961. Cover design by Romek Marber

617. *You and the Refugee*, 1939

618. *The New Poetic*, 1967. Cover design by Germano Facetti

619. *Maigret's Revolver*, 1963. Cover design by Romek Marber

620. *Recorded Jazz: A Critical Guide*, 1958. Cover design by Dennis Bailey

621. *The Real Cost of War*, 1940

622. *The Children of Sanchez*, 1966. The cover shows *Frammento di testa* (oil), by Enrico Colombotto Rosso

623. *The Captain and the Enemy*, 1999. Cover photographs: Theatre – Everett Collection; Screen image– Photofest

624. *War Gaming*, 1970. Cover design by Ian McLaren

625. *Quatermass and the Pit*, 1960. Cover illustration by Bryan Kneale

626. *Penguin Science Survey A: 1965*, 1965. Cover design by Henrion

627. *What's Wrong with British Industry?*, 1964. Cover photograph by Roger Mayne

628. *Disorders of Memory and Learning*, 1968. Cover design by Martin Bassett

629. *Cancer*, 1962. Cover design by Germano Facetti

630. *Mesdames, Messieurs ...*, 1963

631. *Psychiatry To-day*, 1963. Cover design by Germano Facetti

632. *The Go-Between*, 1958. Cover illustration by Lynton Lamb

633. *Supersticiones y Leyendas*, 1947

634. *Penguin Science Survey B: 1965*, 1965. Cover design by Henrion

635. *Murder in Pastiche*, 1962. Cover design by Romek Marber

636. *The Death and Life of Great American Cities*, 1964. Cover design by Germano Facetti

637. *The Rise of the South African Reich*, 1964. Cover design by Gillian Lewis

638. *The Stain on the Snow*, 1964. Cover design by Romek Marber

639. *A Dictionary of Science*, 1971. Cover design by Germano Facetti

640. *Captain Swing*, 1973. Cover design by John McConnell

641. *The Scarlet Letters*, 1965. Cover design by Romek Marber

642. *Such Darling Dodos*, 1968. Cover design by Romek Marber

643. *The Immoralist*, 1981. The cover shows a detail from van Dongen's 'Les Fellans', in the Musée Nationale d'Art Moderne, Paris (Snark International)

644. *The Triple Thinkers*, 1962. Cover design by Germano Facetti

645. *A Portrait of the Artist as a Young Man*, 1968. Cover design by Germano Facetti using photographs from the National Library of Ireland

646. *Nana*, 1985. The cover, designed by Germano Facetti, shows a detail from a nude by Toulouse-Lautrec in the Von der Heydt Museum, Wuppertal.

647. *Tolstoy or Dostoevsky*, 1967. The cover shows 'Red, White and Brown' by Mark Rothko in the Kunstmuseum, Basel (photo Hinz, Basel)

648. *Parables for the Theatre*, 1966. Cover design by Denise York

649. *Hangman's Holiday*, 1962. Cover design by Romek Marber